MAIN

An Actor on the Elizabethan Stage

Titles in The Working Life series include:

THE WORKING LIFE

An Actor on the Elizabethan Stage

STEPHEN CURRIE

LUCENT BOOKS®

THOMSON
—————*—————™
GALE

San Diego • Detroit • New York • San Francisco • Cleveland • New Haven, Conn. • Waterville, Maine • London • Munich

On cover: An artist depicts a scene from William Shakespeare's great tragedy
King Lear, in which the elderly king is visited by his daughter Cordelia.

LIBRARY OF CONGRESS CATALOGING-IN-PUBLICATION DATA

Currie, Stephen, 1960–
    An actor on the Elizabethan stage / by Stephen Currie.
        v. cm. — (The working life series)
Includes bibliographical references and index.
Summary: Discusses various aspects of theatrical life, including staging and perform-
ance, financing, types of acting troupes, and social and economic influences.
Contents: A kind of contradiction—Sharers and apprentices—Hired men—Preparing a
production—The performance—On tour.
    ISBN 1-59018-174-3 (alk. paper)
    1. Theater—England—History—16th century—Juvenile literature. [1. Theater—
England—History—16th century.] I. Title. II. Series.
    PN2589 .C87 2003
    792'.0942'09031—dc21
                                                                            2002009460

CONTENTS

FOREWORD

"The strongest bond of human sympathy outside the family relations should be one uniting all working people of all nations and tongues and kindreds."

Abraham Lincoln. 1864

Work is a common activity in which almost all people engage. It is probably the most universal of human experiences. As Henry Ford, inventor of the Model T said, "There will never be a system invented which will do away with the necessity of work." For many people, work takes up most of their day. They spend more time with their coworkers than family and friends. And the common goals people pursue on the job may be among the first thoughts that they have in the morning, and the last that they may have at night.

While the idea of work is universal, the way it is done and who performs it varies considerably throughout history. The story of work is inextricably tied to the history of technology, the history of culture, and the history of gender and race. When the typewriter was invented, for example, it was considered the exclusive domain of men who worked as secretaries. As women workers became more accepted, the secretarial role was gradually filled by women. Finally, with the invention of the computer, the modern secretary spends little time actually typing correspondence. Files are delivered via computer, and more time is spent on other tasks than the manual typing of correspondence and business.

This is just one example of how work brings together technology, gender, and culture. Another example is the American plantation slave. The harvesting of cotton was initially so cumbersome and time consuming that even with slaves, its profitability was doubtful. With the invention of the cotton gin, however, efficiency improved, and slavery became a viable agricultural tool. It also became a southern tradition and institution, enough that the South was willing to go to war to preserve it.

The books in Lucent's Working Life series strive to show the intermingling of work, and its reflection in culture, technology, race, and gender. Indeed, history viewed through the perspective of the average worker is both enlightening and fascinating. Take the history of the typewriter, mentioned above. Readers today have access to more technology than any of their historical counterparts, and, in fact, though they would find the typewriter's keyboard familiar, they would find using it a bore. Finding out that people spent their days sitting over that machine (with no talk of carpal tunnel syndrome!) and were valued if they made no typing errors because corrections were cumbersome to make and, in some legal professions, made documents invalid, is an interesting story that involves many different aspects of history.

The desire to work is almost innate. As German socialist Ferdinand Lassalle said in the 1850s, "Workingmen we all are so far as we have the desire to make ourselves useful to human society in any way whatever." Yet each historical period offers a million different stories of the history of each job and how it was performed. And that history is the history of human society.

Each book in the Working Life series strives to tell the tale of these anonymous workers. Primary source quotes offer veracity and immediacy to each volume, letting the workers themselves tell their stories. In addition, thorough bibliographies tell students where they can find out more information and complete indexes allow for easy perusal of the text. While students learn about the work of years gone by, they gain empathy for those who toil, and, perhaps, a universal pride in taking up the work that will someday be theirs.

INTRODUCTION

"A KIND OF CONTRADICTION"

Of all the art forms that flourished in Elizabethan England, none was as important or successful as the theater. During the late sixteenth and early seventeenth centuries, plays were seemingly everywhere. Troupes of professional actors performed in fine London theaters and in small provincial town halls alike; playwrights churned out dramas at a remarkable pace. Audiences, in turn, eagerly flocked to see the newest offerings, as well as revivals of the old favorites they had enjoyed in previous years.

The widespread interest in drama stemmed in part from the monarchy itself. Queen Elizabeth I, who reigned from 1558 until her death in 1603, was an avid supporter of the theater. So, too, were her successors to the throne: James I, who ruled from 1603 to 1625, and Charles I, whose reign lasted until 1649. Elizabeth, in particular, enjoyed the company of artistic people and looked with favor on talented actors, playwrights, and musicians. Elizabeth was so vital to the success of theater during her reign that the term "Elizabethan theater" generally includes the dramas written and presented under the reigns of James and Charles as well. Her support and enthusiasm helped to set the tone for the public's focus on the art.

However, despite support from England's monarchs, it was not easy to be a member of an Elizabethan acting troupe. Only a few companies were successful over the long term. The men and boys who made up the troupes—women did not perform—could not simply assume that an eager audience would come to see any play they chose to present. On the contrary, Elizabethan playgoers were notoriously fickle, and their tastes changed frequently. Moreover, competition from other acting companies was usually fierce. The troupes either gave their audience what it wanted, or else they faced bankruptcy.

BEING AN ACTOR

But pleasing the audiences could be a demanding chore. Actors performed six afternoons a week, usually after spending the morning at rehearsals. Moreover, they performed in crowded, open-air theaters that lacked any kind of sound amplification system. And actors needed to memorize more than just one or two scripts at a time. In an effort to at-

tract customers, it was common for troupes to present a different play nearly every day. The records of acting companies show that they frequently presented five separate productions in a week, seven in ten days, or a dozen in a single three-week stretch. The routine was grueling at best and nearly impossible at its worst.

Nor did actors receive the respect of society at large. Despite Elizabeth's official support, many English citizens considered the men who made up the

Queen Elizabeth I was a staunch supporter of theater, which flourished during her reign.

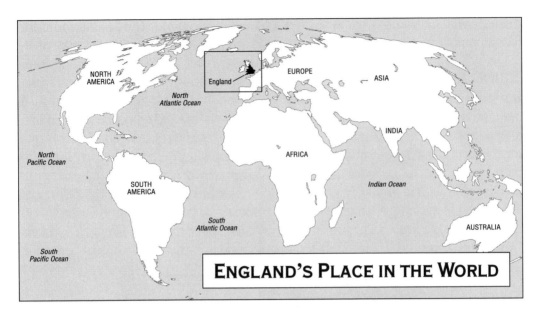

ENGLAND'S PLACE IN THE WORLD

companies to be little better than thieves or tramps. There was considerable religious sentiment, too, against plays in general and theater troupes in particular. Indeed, many Elizabethans attempted to put the acting troupes out of business entirely. As one contemporary writer wittily summed up the situation, "[The actor's] profession has in it a kind of contradiction, for none is more disliked, and yet none more applauded."[1]

Yet, there were definite advantages to being a member of a theatrical troupe. The most talented of the actors achieved a degree of wealth and fame they could not have attained in any other field. The sudden rise of great playwrights, scripts, and actors com-

bined to make the Elizabethan period a wonderfully exciting time to be involved in drama. The men in most of the troupes also enjoyed the camaraderie that developed from working together with intensity and enthusiasm.

And most attractive of all, of course, was the feeling of being onstage in front of an appreciative audience. The sound of applause at the end of a successful production made up for a lot of stress and disapproval. In the end, it was the desire to perform, not a drive for wealth, status, or companionship, that led the actors to join the troupes of the time. The working life of an Elizabethan actor had its share of hardships, but it had its share of joys as well.

CHAPTER 1

SHARERS AND APPRENTICES

At the beginning of Elizabeth's reign, companies of actors—or "players," as they were usually called—were under the sponsorship of a nobleman. Officially, the actors who made up the troupe were household servants, equivalent in rank and status to butlers, footmen, and others in the lord's employ. The names of the theatrical companies reflected the connection between the actors and their noble sponsors: Some of the best-known troupes of the time included the Earl of Leicester's Men, Lord Strange's Men, and Lord Howard's Men.

The link between the players and the nobles was tight. The actors answered to the nobleman and performed where and when he directed. Usually those performances were in the lord's house, but the noblemen sometimes permitted the troupe to give productions for the public as well. In turn, the lord paid the actors for their time and talents. He also

offered them legal protection in case they ran into trouble with the authorities. Unattached actors were subject to

Robert Dudley, the Earl of Leicester, was a patron of the theater and of his own acting troupe.

arrest as tramps, thieves, and vagrants. Noble sponsorship helped the troupes to avoid such a fate.

But as the Elizabethan era continued, the popularity of the theater began to change the way in which theatrical troupes were structured. No longer were audiences willing to wait for a nobleman to authorize his players to entertain outside his estate. Nor were the players willing to continue deferring to their lord in all artistic and economic matters. As a result, by the 1570s the players were beginning to operate independently of the lords.

Technically, nothing much changed. The acting troupes continued to have the sponsorship of their lord. Most of them kept the same names as before, too. But by the second half of Elizabeth's reign, it was difficult to find a nobleman who supported a company of players in the direct way that had been common in the 1550s. The nobles began to function more as figureheads. Both creatively and financially, the troupes were increasingly on their own.

SHARERS

By the late 1570s, acting companies were essentially owned and operated by individual players. These men were usually called "sharers," since each received a share of the company's profits. The number of sharers varied according to the troupe and was not necessarily constant within any given company.

However, most important groups seem to have had somewhere between six and twelve sharers in all. The Lord Admiral's Men, for example, probably had ten sharers in 1598, and Prince Charles's Company had the same number in 1616.

As a rule, the sharers were the best-known and most experienced actors in the troupe. Richard Burbage, who was among the greatest actors in English history, was for many years a sharer of the Lord Chamberlain's Men. Richard Tarlton, another highly respected player, owned a share of the rival Queen's Men from 1583 until his death in 1588. And among the sharers of the Lord Admiral's Men was Edward Alleyn, one of the four or five most famous actors of his time. Indeed, Alleyn was so well known that some Elizabethans referred to his troupe as "Ed. Alleyn's company"[2] rather than by its official title.

However, not all sharers were as known for their acting skills as Alleyn, Burbage, or Tarlton. William Shakespeare, for example, never attained great fame as an actor, yet he was a sharer along with Burbage in the Lord Chamberlain's Men. Another relatively obscure player, Thomas Heywood, shared in the profits of the Worcester–Queen Anne's Company. Both Shakespeare and Heywood were playwrights as well as actors, which may explain why they owned shares in their respective companies; but plenty of sharers were

THE KING'S-CHAMBERLAIN'S-HUNSDON'S-DERBY'S MEN

It can be extremely difficult to trace the histories of many Elizabethan acting troupes. One reason is that their names often changed. As sponsoring lords died or lost interest in the groups they had helped to found, companies—even successful ones—needed to search for different backers. Most of the time, the group changed its name to reflect its new sponsorship.

That was most famously the case with the group with which William Shakespeare was affiliated. The group went through a succession of noble sponsors, including Lord Hunsdon and the earl of Derby, before coming under the control of the Lord Chamberlain, Henry Carey, in 1594. The chamberlain's sponsorship was extremely lucky for the company. Not only was Carey an enthusiastic supporter of plays, but he was responsible for arranging entertainments for the queen. He frequently had his players perform specifically for her, which put the troupe constantly in the public eye and assured their short-term success.

But the company did not remain under the chamberlain's eye for long. After Elizabeth's death in 1603, the troupe's sponsorship was taken over by the new king, James I, and the name was changed to the King's Men in his honor. The group remained among the most respected and talented companies in all England until plays were forbidden altogether later in the century.

William Shakespeare's acting troupe was known as the King's Men.

not distinguished, either as actors or playwrights.

Other sharers had even looser connections with the stage. A few companies had sharers who functioned more as managers than as actors. Since the managerial tasks of a theater were great, it simplified things to have two or three of the sharers do this work. At one point, for instance, the Admiral's Men assigned sharers Robert Shaa and Thomas Downton the task of approving all company payments. The Queen's Men, similarly, gave one sharer the responsibility of buying "the furniture, apparel, and other necessaries."[3]

The time commitments involved in carrying out these managerial tasks often made it difficult for these men to appear onstage. In some cases, the administrative duties rotated. After a year or two, the Admiral's Men replaced Downton with Samuel Rowley. But in other companies, the same sharers held the same posts for many years. It is likely that these sharers were chosen less for their acting abilities and their knowledge of the theater than for their administrative talents.

Finally, some sharers held their posts simply by virtue of personal wealth. William Bankes, for example, paid one hundred pounds—about $30,000 today—to the other sharers of Prince Charles's Men in the early 1630s, thus giving him a voice in the running of the company and a share of the proceeds. So far as is known, Bankes had absolutely no theatrical experience. No doubt he joined in part because he hoped to earn his investment back, but he may also have liked the idea of being around the excitement of the theater. What he brought to the company is easier to measure. One hundred pounds would have purchased costumes, allowed the rental of a bigger theater, or helped to carry the company through hard times.

NEW SHARERS

The list of sharers was not static. To form new companies, sharers simply pooled their money to get the operation going. But if the troupe lasted any length of time, some original members would retire, die, or move on. Then other actors would be invited to take their places. Often, a new recruit would have to put up some of his own money to buy his way in, much as did the nonactor William Bankes. While a few had the money to spare, most were forced to borrow the necessary sum from friends or relatives. In 1595, for instance, an uncle loaned Francis Henslowe nine pounds "to lay down for his half share with the company which he doth play with."[4]

New sharers also had to sign elaborate legal documents specifying their rights and responsibilities toward the company and toward their fellow officers. Some of the clauses explained, for example, that the new sharer had to help purchase props and costumes as the need arose. Others described how and when he could expect to collect his earnings. These parts of the contract were straightforward and would have been common in any legal document of the time. However, not all aspects of the sharers' responsibilities were as simple.

An early seventeenth-century contract binding Robert Dawes to a troupe, for example, listed many ways in which Dawes might fail the company, and spelled out the penalties he would face if he did so. "If he the said Robert Dawes happen to be overcome with drink at the time when he [ought to] play, by the judgment of four of the company," read a typical section, "he shall and will pay ten shillings."[5] (A shilling, in the English monetary system, was equal to 12 pence, or pennies; 20 schillings, in turn, was the same as a pound. Ten shillings in Elizabethan times had roughly the same buying power as about $150 today.) The fine for drunkenness was harsh, but insignificant next to the graver sin of stealing books, props, or costumes that belonged to the company. If Dawes did that, the contract continued, he could expect to pay a forfeit of forty pounds to the other sharers.

In the eyes of the law, the sharers *were* the company. In order for an acting troupe to perform, the Crown had to issue it a patent, or a license, to do business. Licenses were usually given to the sharers, rather than to the noble sponsor or to the company as a whole. The 1603 patent for the Chamberlain's Men, for example, stated:

> "licenced and authorized . . . these our servants Lawrence Fletcher, William Shakespeare, Richard Burbage, Augustine Phillips, John Heminges, Henry Condell, William Sly, Robert Armin, Richard

Acting troupes, such as the one to which Richard Burbage belonged, had to be licensed by the Crown.

Cowley, and the rest of their associates freely to use and exercise the art and faculty of playing comedies, tragedies, histories, interludes, morals, pastorals, stageplays and such others like as they have already studied [learned] or hereafter shall use and study."[6]

The identification of the company with the sharers made sense. The sharers, after all, put their own money into the troupe. They were responsible for buying set pieces, renting theaters, and paying the craftsmen who created costumes and props. They got rich if the company did well, and they lost their investments if the company did poorly. By the middle of Elizabeth's reign, it was they, and not their noble sponsors, who stood to gain or to lose depending on the success or failure of the companies.

FINANCIAL SUCCESSES

Under the best circumstances, the sharers prospered. If companies drew full houses and managed to accumulate a large stock of costumes, props, and set pieces, the sharers split substantial sums of money. In 1598, a sharer in the Queen's Men could expect to earn as much as twenty-six shillings a week, enough to enable a

---

∂ ADMISSION FEES AND ECONOMICS ∂

While a noble sponsor might provide his company with an emergency loan or even an outright gift from time to time, the great bulk of a theater troupe's income was from admission fees. Thus, the bigger the audience, the greater the troupe's income. However, the company did not keep all the gate receipts. Instead, they divided the proceeds with the owners of the theaters in which the troupe performed. The precise percentages were open to negotiation, but successful troupes were generally able to keep at least half of the money for themselves. The company's share was then divided among the sharers, either weekly or after every performance.

Both theater owners and players occasionally complained about the system. Each side charged that the division was unfair and made it impossible for them to turn a profit. Indeed, there is evidence that some theater owners did cheat actors out of some of the money that was rightfully theirs. (The reverse may have been true as well.) But that was less a problem with the idea of dividing the money than an issue of criminal behavior. On the whole, the arrangement seems to have worked out relatively well for both sides.

man to live comfortably. In 1640, the total value of one company was estimated at 3,000 pounds—an enormous amount for the time.

Certainly the sharers did better, as a rule, than most other Elizabethans. Some craftsmen and most merchants could expect to make the sort of money that a successful sharer could command. Ordinary uneducated workers, though, could not. Neither could many among the ranks of those who were quite well educated. Writers, for example, made far less money than sharers. One jealous author called acting "the most excellent vocation in the world for money." [7]

Indeed, a handful of sharers became very wealthy. Foremost among them was Edward Alleyn of the Lord Admiral's Men. Alleyn's fortune was substantially increased by careful investment in land and by a host of other moneymaking activities. However, he began with nothing but his share of the proceeds from his acting troupe. It helped that Alleyn had perhaps the best reputation of any actor in England during the Elizabethan period. Audiences flocked to see him perform, swelling the gate receipts and enriching him and his fellow sharers. As one contemporary put it, no classical actor "could ever perform more in action than famous Ned Alleyn." [8]

Still, even if wealth was not a realistic goal for most sharers, many of them were financially comfortable. The most

successful, conceded a contemporary writer who did not think much of actors, were "honest householders and citizens well thought of among their neighbors at home." [9] Henry Condell of the Chamberlain's Men, for example, was one of many wealthy enough to afford a servant. Nearly all sharers were married; most had children. William Shakespeare was probably the only sharer in the Chamberlain's Company who did not own property in London. The rest owned homes in comfortable, middle-class areas of the city.

In fact, many of the most important sharers were not only well-to-do, they were also active in civic affairs. Henry Condell was a warden of the local parish church. Edward Alleyn helped to found a school. Nicholas Tooley of the King's Men directed that much of his money should go to charitable causes when he died. They were not the only actors who were solid, influential members of the community. As one historian writes, these sharers were "exactly the sort of people that the mayor of London would have approved of thoroughly if he could have brought himself to approve of actors at all." [10]

Despite official disapproval, the best-known sharers of Elizabethan times were as close to being celebrities as any nonroyal person of the period. According to historian M.C. Bradbrook, Richard Tarlton was "a national figure, the first actor to achieve stardom, [and] perhaps the first man to be known all

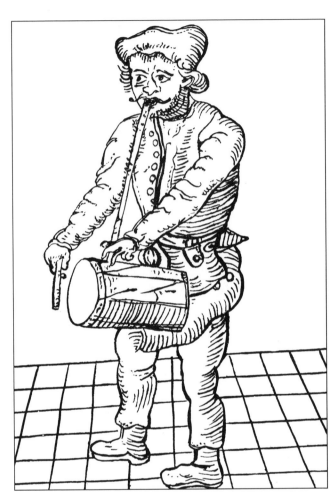

Richard Tarlton was the first Elizabethan actor to achieve national fame and popularity.

over England simply in terms of his personality."[11] A satirical play of the time included the line: "He's not counted a gentleman that knows not Dick [Richard] Burbage and Will Kempe"[12]; Kempe, like Burbage, was a sharer and a successful actor with the Lord Chamberlain's troupe.

MONETARY CONCERNS

Most sharers were not nearly as successful, however. Companies failed fre-

quently during the Elizabethan period. Theatrical troupes of the time formed and disappeared with great speed. Some were absorbed by more powerful rivals, while others simply vanished. A company called Lord Abergavenny's Men, for example, opened in 1571 and dissolved in 1576; Sir Robert Lane's Men only performed between summer 1570 and early 1572. A company called Lord Vaux's Men seems to have lasted for less than a full year. When a troupe went out of business, its sharers sold off the remaining properties, costumes, and other assets, and tried to join another company elsewhere.

In many cases, the fault of the bankruptcy lay with the sharers themselves. Sometimes they were too hasty in forming a group, or not careful enough to make sure that theater owners and suppliers were not taking advantage of them. "He hath broken and dismembered five companies,"[13] complained one set of sharers about a theater owner. The details of the "dismemberment" are lost, but it seems likely that the men who ran the bankrupt troupes were not as careful as they might have been when it came to signing contracts or determining the actual proceeds from each performance.

Even established companies could make bad decisions. For a period of almost eight years, the Queen's Men entrusted their financial dealings to one sharer, Christopher Beeston. They empowered Beeston to act on the company's behalf "without the . . . direction or knowledge"[14] of any other sharer. When money ran low, the other sharers accused Beeston of embezzlement, and the company soon collapsed.

But forces over which the sharers had no control also affected financial security. Economic depressions, for example, usually cut dramatically into the size of theatrical audiences. Epidemics, too, usually resulted in the closing of the theaters for public health reasons.

When times were hard, the largest and best-known companies occasionally received grants to help tide them over. In 1603, King James gave Richard Burbage thirty pounds "for the maintenance and relief of himself and the rest of his company."[15] Smaller companies, however, rarely received any money at all; and even thirty pounds was not enough to compensate Burbage and his fellow sharers for a lost season.

Whatever the reason, sharers often found themselves in desperate financial straits. Their options in such cases were limited. To forestall bankruptcy,

King James (pictured) provided Richard Burbage and his acting troupe with financial support in 1603.

some sharers borrowed from money-lenders, using the company's assets as collateral. Borrowing, however, was risky. A few of the larger companies could manage to pay back the principal as well as the accumulated interest. Smaller companies, though, often went out of business before they could pay off the loan.

The most famous of these lenders was Philip Henslowe, a London entrepreneur with strong ties to the theatrical world. Among Henslowe's many loans to acting troupes was a series of four loans he made to the Admiral's Men in the spring of 1596. The Admiral's sharers, however, struggled mightily to pay him back. Because of poor crowds and unexpected expenses, by the end of the year they had repaid Henslowe only two of the thirty-five pounds they had borrowed from him.

Other companies, facing possible bankruptcy, pawned or sold their costumes and props. Without these, of course, performance was impossible. In these cases, the sharers could hope that some money would be left over after all debts were paid. Sometimes that was the case. More often, though, it was not. Thomas Towne of the Admiral's Men was forced to pawn a pair of his own stockings in 1602 to make ends meet, and his situation was hardly unique. Sharers hoped to avoid the fate of John Lowin, who held a stake in Worcester's Men at the end of Elizabeth's reign, but

"died very old . . . and his poverty was as great as his age."[16]

BECOMING A SHARER

There was no one path into the theater for the men who became sharers. Many of the most famous were originally tradesmen: "men of occupations," as one observer of the time put it, "which they have forsaken to live by playing."[17] The connection between trades and the theater made sense. Before Elizabeth ascended to the throne, plays were often performed by small groups of craftsmen, amateurs who put on productions in their spare time. By the Elizabethan era, theater had become much more professionalized. Such off-the-cuff productions were far less common. Nevertheless, there was a long tradition of acting among the tradesmen of London, and the tradition persisted into Elizabethan times and beyond.

Little is known about the early years of most sharers, but it is not hard to find men whose earliest training was in the trades. Robert Armin of the Chamberlain's Men started as a goldsmith's apprentice, while Martin Slater of the Admiral's Men was an ironmonger. Ben Jonson was listed in official documents as "citizen and bricklayer of London"[18] long after he had laid his last brick. As for James Burbage, the father of Richard, he was "by occupation a joiner," an observer reported. However, "reaping but a small

❧ RELATIONS BETWEEN SHARERS ❧

In the most successful companies, there was a strong and lasting connection between the men who ran the troupe. The depth of the link can often be seen in the wills of the players who served as sharers. John Heminges of the King's Men, for example, left money to buy rings for each of his fellow sharers. Another King's player, Augustine Phillips, went further. "I give and bequeath unto my fellow [sharer] William Shakespeare a 30s [shilling] piece in gold," he wrote, as quoted in Wickham, Berry, and Ingram, *English Professional Theatre, 1530–1660;* Phillips's will then continued through the list of all the other sharers of his company, giving each a share of his estate.

However, not all sharers maintained such a high regard for one another. Squabbling among the leaders of a troupe was common. Some of the worst disagreements took place when one sharer wished to leave the organization. In good times, the remaining sharers were more than happy to buy a colleague out at a fair price; one man asked for fifty pounds and got it. In bad times, however, the actors who ran the company often disputed the value of the share. Lawsuits were usually the result.

Other sharers fell out for different reasons. When William Bankes bought his way into Prince Charles's Company, he quickly ran into difficulties with the other sharers. In a lawsuit, he complained that they had charged him too much for the purchase of costumes. He also argued that they had not paid him his full share of the proceeds. The others denied it, and added their opinion that Bankes had injured the company by holding back funds he owed the company. He "hath broken the same orders [that is, the rules] by his disorderly behavior," they complained, as quoted in Bentley, *The Profession of Player in Shakespeare's Time,* "to the very great prejudice of said company."

living by the same, gave it over and became a common player."[19]

Although much about the career path of individual sharers is unknown, it seems clear that most were players by the time they were in their late teens or early twenties. Except for the few who came to the companies through their managerial talents or their wealth, virtually all successful sharers were veteran actors before achieving the status of sharer. Those who joined companies during their late twenties or beyond would have had difficulty learning their craft in so short a time.

That was especially true because becoming a professional actor involved intensive training. Elizabethan players needed to develop many different skills before they could be comfortable on stage. Many plays included dances, for instance, so aspiring actors had to learn dance steps and movements. Sword fighting was another necessity. The characters in Elizabethan dramas often fenced, and audiences could be deeply critical of actors whose moves did not seem sufficiently polished. And acrobatics were important, too; most actors had to learn tumbling skills.

More significantly, players had to learn the craft of acting. How to hold their bodies, how to move on stage, how to memorize their lines—all of these were skills that did not come naturally to most young men. Vocal projection was a particular issue. It was not possible during Elizabethan times to amplify voices through the use of microphones, so actors of the period had to learn to exaggerate their speech to be heard over the largest of crowds. As one historian expressed it, "It was not the physical activity that caught and held the emotions of the audience; it was the words."[20] A play was nothing if the words went unheard.

Elizabethan actors were required to be adept swordsmen, as are their modern counterparts in this 1949 film production of Shakespeare's Hamlet.

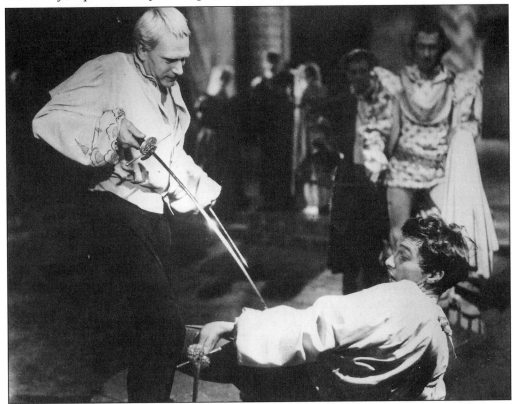

APPRENTICESHIPS

Because the training process was so involved, it made sense to begin early. Thus, many of the sharers began their careers as apprentice actors. That was especially true of those born in the 1570s and beyond, but even those of earlier generations sometimes were brought up in show business. England had a long tradition of boys' choirs, some of which performed short plays as well, and generations of boys had been apprenticed to these choirs. From there it was a short step to the use of boys as apprentices in theatrical troupes.

The use of these boys, however, was controversial. The concern was not that apprentices would be overworked or otherwise exploited. The Elizabethan era was a time when children were expected to contribute to society in any way they could. The objection, instead, was moral. Those who opposed the production of plays feared that the apprentices would be doomed to a life in the theater. Too many of the era's players, mourned Stephen Gosson in 1579, had been "trained up from their childhood to this abominable exercise, and have now no other way to get their living."[21]

Beyond educational purposes, there was another reason for having apprentices in Elizabethan acting troupes. English convention of the time forbade women from appearing on stage. The tradition, instead, was to have all female parts played by boys. Most playwrights of the period avoided writing substantial roles for women, but it was hard to eliminate female parts altogether. Shakespeare, in fact, made many of his most important characters women. Pivotal roles such as Desdemona in *Othello,* Rosalind in *As You Like It,* and Miranda in *The Tempest* are invariably played by women today, but were performed by boys when the dramas first were presented.

To modern audiences, the notion of casting boys as girls, let alone women, seems peculiar and probably ineffective. But that was not the way Elizabethans saw it. To them, it was perfectly reasonable to have a preteen boy playing a twenty-year-old girl and another playing her elderly grandmother. Nor was it odd to have a young man in the part of Romeo and a somewhat younger boy playing opposite him as Juliet. Using boys in female roles was simply the convention, and audiences accepted it without complaint.

It helped that the staging for these scenes generally involved little physical contact. In the famous balcony scene from *Romeo and Juliet,* the two lovers never come close to touching; words, rather than gestures, demonstrate the depth of their connection, and Shakespeare wrote the play that way deliberately. Moreover, leading female roles would have been given to the best and most experienced apprentices. But there is no doubt that the actors were effective, sex and age notwithstanding. "The

In sixteenth-century theater all female roles were assumed by boys. Here, mirroring that convention in a nineteenth-century gender twist, two actresses play the roles of Romeo and Juliet.

stage's jewel,"[22] Ben Jonson called child actor Salomon Pavy.

RECRUITING BOYS

The theatrical apprenticeships worked much like other apprenticeships of the time. Just as an aspiring printer would work in a print shop for several years under the supervision of a master printer, so too did prospective actors labor

and learn under the tutelage of the company's sharers. The boys were thus apprenticed not to the company itself, but to the individual actors. Indeed, they were usually referred to by the name of their master, as for example "Robinson's boy," "Thomas Downton's bigger boy," or "Mr. Denygten's little boy."[23]

In most cases, the apprenticeship seems to have been fairly straightforward. A boy's family bound him over to a sharer for a specified period of time. The exact amount of time varied considerably, depending mainly on the boy's age. Abel Cooke, for example, was apprenticed to Thomas Kendall of the Queen's Revels Company "for and during the sum of three years."[24] Arthur Savill, on the other hand, was apprenticed for eight years, and John Heminges of the Chamberlain's Men took on William Trigg for a twelve-year term.

Generally, too, apprenticeship contracts spelled out the rights and responsibilities of both sides to the agreement. Boys did not receive cash for their work; any wages they were due went to the sharer who was responsible for them. But the apprentices were entitled to food, housing, and the training to prepare them for a life in the theater. In exchange, the boys agreed to do as they were instructed. Whether they were happy with the arrangement or not, the sharers and their families were, and in legal terms that was all that mattered.

In a few cases, apprenticeships were more complicated. The boys' choirs were sponsored by both the royal family and by the Anglican Church, and choir leaders were authorized to impress boys—that is, to force boys to sing in the choirs, taking them off the street if necessary. Several sharers adopted this tradition, though without official backing. In 1601, a London man complained that Nathaniel Giles of the Blackfriars had impressed his son and forced him to join "a company of lewd and dissolute mercenary players."[25] The boy was eventually returned to his father's custody.

Some boys, too, were mistreated, grew homesick, or otherwise had difficulty managing life in the troupe. Abel Cooke, for instance, left his master after only six months. The master sued his mother to have the apprenticeship revoked, but Mrs. Cooke objected. In the end they agreed to return Abel to his master, and his mother signed an extra contract stating that her son would not "depart, absent, or prolong himself from the said service and practice and playing without the consent and license"[26] of his master.

CONNECTIONS

However, the bulk of evidence suggests that Cooke's example was unusual. Surviving records tend to support the notion that the relationships between masters and apprentices were strong. Many of the apprentices took great

pains to remember and thank the sharers who had devoted such time and energy to them. Some even thanked the sharers' wives, many of whom had played a large role in raising and instructing the boys. In his will, Nicholas Tooley left ten pounds to the widow of Richard Burbage, his former master, "as a remembrance of my love [and] in respect of her motherly care over me."[27]

In turn, the sharers recognized the value of their apprentices. "I give to Samuel Gilborne," wrote Augustine Phillips in his will, "my late [former] apprentice, the sum of forty shillings, and my mouse-colored velvet hose, and a white taffeta doublet, a black taffeta suit, my purple cloak, sword, and dagger, and my bass viol."[28] Phillips was far from the only sharer who took pains to recognize and reward his former apprentices for their hard work.

It is unlikely that all apprentices went on to become actors as adults. Many must have found the life too hard, their talents too meager, or the fellowship dull. And some, such as Salomon Pavy, died before they had served out their apprenticeships. However, many boy actors did continue in the field. Stephen Hammerton, an observer reported, "was at first a most noted and beautiful woman actor [an apprentice], but afterwards he acted with equal grace and applause, a young lover's part [a romantic lead, played by a man]."[29] William Ostler,

❧ FOOD ❧

Like the rest of their countrymen, members of Elizabethan acting troupes ate a somewhat heavy and monotonous diet. Breakfasts were large and usually consisted of bread and cheese, along with various kinds of meat and salted fish. There was also a kind of stew called pottage, which was made from beef or lamb. The meal would be washed down with beer, wine, or ale.

Around noon, Elizabethans sat down for dinner. This meal included more or less the same combination of food as was provided for breakfast, and usually in the same amounts. The actors, however, probably ate less at dinner than did the average workingman of the time. They performed in the afternoons, and eating a full meal shortly before going onstage would have made the players sluggish.

The third and last meal of the day was supper. It differed from breakfast and dinner only in that it tended to be somewhat lighter; otherwise, the foods were basically the same. The actors, however, may well have eaten a correspondingly larger supper than most other Elizabethans, since they had cut back on their dinners.

By modern standards, the diet was rather unappealing; but then, the Elizabethans did not have many options. Many foods common today were unknown to Europeans in the sixteenth and early seventeenth century. Tea, coffee, tomatoes, chocolate, corn, and many other foods were either unavailable or scarce and expensive. Nor could Elizabethans store food easily. Although people of the time grew apples, carrots, pears, spinach, and several other fruits and vegetables, they were usually added to the diet only when they were in season.

In any case, the Elizabethan actors lived in a time when famine was always a possibility. They were too glad to have food to waste much time grumbling about what they were served.

Nathan Field, and Nicholas Tooley likewise all began as apprentices and had long and successful acting careers afterward.

The lives of apprentices and sharers were far from easy. Even the best-known and most popular acting troupes of Elizabethan England were often only a plague outbreak or a bad managerial decision away from disaster. There is no doubt that many gave up on the profession and went into other lines of work instead. But those who stayed seem to have genuinely enjoyed their lives. They *were* the company, and they made the most of their opportunity.

CHAPTER 2

HIRED MEN

Sharers and apprentices were the most important members of Elizabethan acting troupes. But they did not make up the entire company. Virtually all plays of the period required more actors and more technical assistance than the sharers and apprentices could manage alone. Thus, Elizabethan troupes included a third class of actor, known as the hired man.

As the name suggests, hired men were employed by the sharers, usually for a term of a year or two, and paid a small weekly wage for their work. According to Roger Clarke of the Queen's Men, the sharers of his troupe "agreed to give unto me six shillings a week so long as I should continue their hired servant." [30] Clarke's salary was common for the period. Records of the time indicate that hired men were paid, on average, between five and ten shillings a week—enough to earn a meager living.

However, the terms of the contract were not always followed. The salaries of the hired men were contingent upon the troupe's success. Sometimes, charged hired man Richard Baxter, "the gettings of the company [were] so small that . . . they did pay unto the hired men or servants no wages and sometimes half wages and sometimes less." [31] The hired men had no recourse for this mistreatment, other than to leave and find a better offer. They had no financial stake in the troupe and no input in the running of the company.

Nor were hired men well respected among the citizens of London. While the well-to-do grudgingly accepted some of the most successful sharers into polite society, the hired men were viewed as scarcely any better than thieves and beggars. Worse, they put on airs. The hired men, wrote observer Stephen Gosson in his anti-theater book,

School of Abuse, "jet under gentlemen's noses in suits of silk . . . [and] look askance over the shoulder at every man, of whom the Sunday before they begged an alms."[32]

Even the sharers did not treat them with the same respect they extended to each other. Surviving cast lists from Elizabethan plays designate sharers as "Mister," while hired men were listed without any title. In a cast list for Thomas Heywood's play *The Fair Maid of the West,* for example, a character called Mullisheg is played by "Mr. Will[iam] Allen," while an unnamed English Merchant is played by "Rob[ert] Axell."[33] In the hierarchy of the theater, the "Mr." was an obvious reminder that Allen was a sharer, and that Axell was not.

The number of hired men varied from company to company, and probably from season to season as well. There was a strong financial incentive for the sharers to keep the number as low as possible: Fewer hired men cost less in salary. On the other hand, more members of the company meant less work for everyone else. Probably the largest number of hired men during the period belonged to the King's Company, among the wealthiest and best known of the acting troupes. At one point the troupe had twenty-one men on its payroll. Most other companies, however, would have had far fewer.

THE MEN

Less is known today about the hired men than about the sharers and the apprentices. Part of the reason is that the hired men were relatively inconspicuous. Unlike the sharers, who played the leads, or the apprentices, who were given important female roles, hired men typically were assigned the smallest parts on stage. With a few exceptions, their roles were little noticed and gave them no chance to shine. Hired men also did a great deal of offstage work. Their labors made the show possible, but they got little credit for it.

Because so little is known about individual hired men, it is difficult to draw broad conclusions about their lives. For some, being a hired man was simply a step on the road to becoming a sharer. Most young actors were not ready to become sharers immediately after finishing their apprenticeships. Artistically and financially, they needed time to grow. These men served as hired men to gain further experience and the recognition and respect of others in the profession. John Lowin, for example, served as a hired man with the King's Men, and Theophilus Bird did the same for Queen Henrietta's Company; both later became sharers.

Some of the hired men, however, were probably new to the theatrical world. Trained originally in another profession, they turned to the acting companies hoping to find a better or more interesting way to support them-

❧ HIRED MEN FOR LIFE ❧

At least a few of the hired men remained in that position during their entire working lives. A player named John King, for example, served as a hired man with the Red Bull Company for thirty years. It is not known whether King simply lacked any ambition to be a sharer, or whether he was held back by a lack of funds, a reputation for unreliability, or an abrasive personality. However, it is clear that he was a valued member of his troupe during those thirty years.

King was primarily an actor, and so, no doubt, were several other hired men who spent their entire careers in that capacity. Most of those who served for years as hired men, though, were specialists whose primary responsibility did not involve acting at all. The musicians, for example, frequently spent much of their working lives as hired men for one company or another. So did the tiremen, or wardrobe keepers.

It helped that musicians and tiremen both had other ways of earning income. Capable instrumentalists were much in demand for nontheatrical performances in Elizabethan England, and most wardrobe keepers had training as tailors. In recognition of these men's potential for earning money elsewhere, the troupes probably paid them better wages than the minor actors received. Moreover, the musicians and tiremen could supplement their incomes when time permitted: Musicians played for parties and feasts, and the wardrobe keepers did tailoring on the side. Because these workers could earn a reasonable living as hired men, they were content to stay in that role for many years.

A 1672 book illustration of the Red Bull playhouse reveals the simplicity of Elizabethan stage settings.

selves. Contemporary lists of hired men include a number of people, such as Nicholas Underhill of the King's Men, who are not known to have been apprentices and seem never to have been sharers, either. It is likely that many of these hired men did not last long in their positions. The work of a hired man was hard, and the pay was low.

MINOR PARTS

Probably the most important part of a hired man's job was to act minor roles in plays. On the surface, this would seem to be a fairly easy task. In Shakespeare's play *The Tempest,* for example, the Shipmaster is given two lines; the character appears on stage for no more than a minute or two. Other small parts in Elizabethan plays required no solo lines at all, merely an appearance as a soldier or a townsperson in a crowd scene. The opening scene of *The Tempest* also calls for several mariners, who come onstage briefly and say in unison: "All lost! To prayers, to prayers! All lost!" [34] None of these parts would be in any way a burden to learn or to perform.

However, the job was not so straightforward. Plays of the period typically required many more minor parts than there were actors available to fill them. John Webster's *The Duchess of Malfi,* for example, calls for several speaking characters who appear in only a scene or two, and an undetermined number of nonspeaking "Madmen, Pilgrims,

Executioners, Officers, Attendants, etc.," [35] all of whom would have been played by hired men. Most troupes of the time did not have enough hired men to fill even those roles.

As a result, minor actors were generally expected to play more than one part per play. The men assigned the role of the mariners in *The Tempest,* for example, would also have been expected to play unnamed Reapers or Spirits, crowd parts that appear briefly later in the work; they might also have taken on small speaking roles such as the lords Francisco and Adrian. This procedure, known as doubling, was standard in Elizabethan times. Playwrights became creative in crafting their scripts to use the smallest possible number of players. One anonymous author proudly demonstrated how only eleven actors could perform the twenty-two parts in his play *Fair Maid of the Exchange;* and an audience member recorded that he had seen Shakespeare's *Julius Caesar,* with more than thirty listed parts, acted by only fifteen people.

Doubling made sound financial sense, and because the parts involved were small, the custom did not affect the play's artistic integrity. The process, however, was not easy on the players. That was especially true because the term "doubling" was something of an understatement. Minor actors were often asked to play five, six, or even more roles in a play. "In one of [Edward] Alleyn's productions," writes historian Marchette Chute, "a single actor played a Tartar nobleman, a spirit, an attendant, a hostage, a ghost, a child, a captain, and a Persian." [36]

DIFFICULTIES OF DOUBLING

Although none of the individual parts proved difficult in itself, the need to play so many in a single work was a major task. Hired men had to do their best to distinguish the characters, no matter how minor. A nobleman, a ghost, and a child would neither look nor sound identical, and finding ways to differentiate them was not necessarily easy. Although most of these actors did not need to learn many lines, they were expected to memorize an assortment of

♪ THE PURITANS ♭

The Puritan Church was a very strict Christian sect with a deep contempt for all things frivolous and immoral. In Puritan eyes, participating in any sinful activity would lead a person directly to damnation. Although most mainstream Christians of the time thought the same way, the Puritans had a much broader definition of what constituted sin than did most other denominations. To them, dancing was a sin; so was music. So, for that matter, was doing much of anything on a Sunday other than praying and attending church.

Plays were high on the Puritan list of sinful behaviors. Attending them was bad enough, but acting in them was worse. In the minds of the Puritans, plays included a multitude of evils. Members of the religion disliked the custom of having boys play women's parts, complaining that God did not intend such a blurring of the line between the genders. They disapproved of the bright and colorful costumes the actors wore, preferring muted grays and darker, more somber colors than were found in the theater. The content of the plays also troubled most Puritans. Elizabethan dramas tended to deal with secular and historical topics, rather than dramatizing stories from the Bible.

During Elizabeth's time Puritans were a minority within England, but the group was loud and numerous enough to have an impact on English society. The Puritans did their best to impose their values and morality on the rest of the nation, and the official tolerance of acting troupes scandalized many influential ministers and other Puritan leaders. They fulminated against the companies from their pulpits and did their best to get the theaters closed down and the players' licenses withdrawn. They were the troupes' strongest and most ferocious opponents—and at the end of King Charles's reign they would succeed, at least temporarily, in putting the theatrical companies out of business.

cues, movements, and reactions. To be able to remember which character entered, and when, required excellent concentration and a prodigious memory.

Worse, each part came with its own costume. A mariner would hardly wear the same clothing as a lord or a reaper. Unfortunately, changing from one outfit to another was tiring and time consuming. Moreover, minor actors were usually under pressure to make their changes as fast as possible. The action on stage continued even as they struggled out of one costume and into the next. It is likely that hired men often were late for entrances, or arrived onstage with their costumes not fully in place.

The biggest issue, though, was the sheer number of parts a minor player had to learn. Since Elizabethan troupes might present twenty or more plays during a single year, the parts quickly mounted up. A hired man could conceivably memorize up to a hundred parts to perform a year's worth of plays. The next year, he might be responsible for learning another thirty.

Certainly, not every hired man played only the secondary roles. From time to time, an especially capable actor might be given a leading part even though he was not a sharer. Richard Alleyn of the Admiral's Men, for example, was assigned one of the title roles in a play called *Frederick and Basilea* when it appeared in 1597, although he was only a hired man. Alleyn, however,

would soon become a sharer. In his case, the leading role seems to have been a sort of audition, allowing the existing sharers to see whether he was prepared to take on more responsibilities within the troupe.

MUSICIANS

Music was an important component of Elizabethan life, and it was therefore a major part of the plays of the time as well. "I have gone to plays more for music sake than for action,"[37] says a character in a contemporary story. While most audience members probably were more enthusiastic about the action, music was nevertheless a major draw. Elizabethans expected to hear good music in the theater, and the acting troupes did their best to meet their audience's expectations.

Much of the theater music of the period was vocal. Elizabethan actors were expected to be able to sing, and many surviving scripts of the period include song lyrics. Often the lead actors did the singing. The spirit Ariel in *The Tempest,* for example, has several short songs scattered throughout the play. But hired men also sang, especially in short group numbers. In the second act of Shakespeare's *A Midsummer Night's Dream,* for example, the chorus of fairies sings a lullaby to their queen Titania.

Instruments were important as well. The men of the Chamberlain's Company, for instance, were expected not only to act but also to "attend [the audi-

Music was an important element in the English theater. The character Ariel (left, in a contemporary production) sings several songs in Shakespeare's The Tempest.

ence] with their fiddles."[38] While sharers and apprentices sometimes played instrumental music, the bulk of this work seems to have gone to the hired men. In part, this was because their acting parts were smaller and less critical, so they could more easily be spared from the stage. It would seem peculiar if a lead player broke character to pick up a viol and accompany a dance; a hired man, in contrast, could just add the music to a long list of other responsibilities.

SPECIALIZATION

Other hired men, however, were in the company less for their acting skills than for their musicianship: They had been brought into the troupe specifically as instrumentalists. These men occasionally appeared onstage between musical cues, especially in nonspeaking roles during crowd scenes. Still, their primary role was as instrumentalists. Large companies may have had six, seven, or even more men who served

A musician is partially visible at center in this modern staging of Romeo and Juliet. *Music in Elizabethan theater was used to great effect in advancing the action, setting a mood, and accompanying dancers.*

more or less full-time as musicians. Smaller companies had, of course, correspondingly fewer; still, most London troupes had at least a couple of men whose primary responsibility was music rather than acting.

Whether primarily actors or musicians, the hired men played a variety of instruments. Stage directions of the time often called for trumpet flourishes: "Horns winded within,"[39] reads a typical direction from *A Midsummer Night's Dream.* Occasionally drums would be heard as well, along with a wind instrument called the hautboy, an early version of today's oboe. And stringed instruments, such as lutes and fiddles, were a part of every major production.

"Lent unto Richard Jones the 22nd of December 1598 to buy a bass viol . . . for the company," wrote Philip Henslowe, "40 shillings."[40]

Elizabethan acting troupes used music in several different ways. Sometimes the music was presented for its own sake. Plays were often preceded by short concerts and followed in the same way. Instrumentalists also played during scene breaks or to accompany dancers. Frequently, though, the music was a central part of the action; it established a mood or advanced the plot. *The Tempest,* for example, includes "solemn and strange music"[41] during a scene of magical events, and a character in *A Midsummer Night's Dream* calls for music to put other characters to sleep.

The line between being part of the action and accompanying it was sometimes thin in Elizabethan plays. Even musicians who had little acting talent wound up onstage—in the part of musicians. The second scene of Thomas Heywood's *A Woman Killed with Kindness,* for example, calls for the entrance of several named characters along with "two or three musicians."[42] During the scene, the characters debate which dance tune they will ask the musicians to play for their entertainment, and the instrumentalists eventually play as the other characters dance. Shakespeare's *Romeo and Juliet* is another example of a play in which genuine musicians assume the onstage role of instrumentalists.

TIREMEN

Costumes were another area in which hired men often served as specialists. Elizabethan acting troupes needed plenty of costumes, most of them extremely ornate. Although historical plays were typically performed in standard Elizabethan dress, a wide variety of costumes was necessary. Acting companies needed armor for soldiers, gowns for queens and duchesses, and everyday clothing for tradespeople. Because the costumes were so important, most troupes hired experienced tailors to look after them.

The exact duties of these wardrobe keepers, or tiremen, varied somewhat from one company to the next. In some troupes, the wardrobe keepers were the ones responsible for creating new costumes. "Paid unto the tireman for the making of the devil's suit," wrote moneylender Philip Henslowe in 1602, "the sum of 10 [shillings] 9 [pence]."[43] In other companies, costumes were purchased—especially fancy royal robes, which could sometimes be bought from the servants of lords and ladies who had died—or commissioned from tailors who were not regular employees of the troupe.

Regardless of the origin of the costumes, all tiremen were responsible for keeping careful track of their companies' wardrobes. Constant performances were hard on the clothing, especially when the weather was hot or rainy, and minor repairs were always needed. Costumers thus had to be adept with needle and thread. Moreover, when an expensive outfit was damaged beyond repair, it was seldom discarded. As costumes intended for leading players lost their finery, the tiremen reworked them into outfits for less important actors. A single piece of material might start off as a king's robe, then see duty as a shepherd's cloak, a pageboy's shirt, and a nobleman's belt as it gradually grew more threadbare. It was up to the tiremen to decide when—and how—to make the changes.

The wardrobe keepers were also constrained by the troupe's financial resources. Costumes cost so much money that most historians agree that costuming was a theatrical troupe's greatest single expense. Creating a fine outfit from scratch required a great deal of time and labor. Moreover, the taffetas, velvets, and other fancy cloths that audiences demanded were hardly cheap. The black satin required to make a suit for a play called *The Black Dog,* Henslowe recorded, cost five pounds, two shillings—an enormous sum of money in Elizabethan times. Tiremen had to be creative with the costumes, but at the same time they needed to try to keep their expenditures from bankrupting the company.

Like musicians, wardrobe keepers sometimes filled in on stage if an extra actor was needed. As one example, a tireman appeared as an attendant in a 1590 play called *The Dead Man's Fortune.* Like the musicians, too, they also occasionally played themselves. The opening of a 1603 play called *The Malcontent* calls for several actors to walk onto the stage. According to the script, one makes his entrance with "a Tire-man following him with a stool." [44] The tireman was given three speeches, none especially long, and then left the stage for the rest of the play. In all likelihood, an actual wardrobe keeper took the part.

A sampling of mid-sixteenth-century fashion. Although actors typically wore standard Elizabethan dress, the wardrobe keepers were kept busy creating a wide variety of elaborate costumes.

❧ GATHERERS ❧

A few hired men served as gatherers, or boxholders. These men were responsible for collecting the admission fees from the audience. Since companies survived almost exclusively on these receipts, gathering was a vital job. Sometimes sharers took on this task when companies were on tour, but in London it was much more usual to pay a hired man to do the work.

Not all gatherers were men, however. Although women had virtually no place within the Elizabethan theater, it was sometimes possible for a woman to work in this capacity. Several actors secured boxholder positions for their wives, and one, Henry Condell, specified in his will that his servant Elizabeth Wheaton should continue in that post for as long as she wanted. Exactly why it was acceptable for a woman to collect money, but not act, sing, or work with costumes, is not known.

The work of a gatherer was not especially hard. There was little physical exertion involved, and gatherers would be finished with their work soon after the show began. This schedule allowed male boxholders to appear on stage in later scenes, or to help with costumes and the like. However, if audience members tried to sneak in without paying, gatherers had to serve as security guards. Sometimes fights broke out. In one case, a gatherer actually killed an unruly customer outside the theater.

The work was sensitive, too, since it involved money. The temptation to cheat must have been strong, and more than one gatherer did slide some of the proceeds into his pocket. Palgrave's Men, for example, fired a boxholder named John Russell in 1617. "Notwithstanding his . . . oaths," wrote an observer, as quoted in Chambers's *The Elizabethan Stage*, "he hath taken the box [the money collected], and many times most unconscionably gathered [it for himself], for which we have resolved he shall never more come to the door [to collect money]."

PROMPTERS

Other hired men served the companies as prompters, sometimes referred to as plotters or book holders. Then as now, the prompter was responsible for feeding lines to a performer who had forgotten what to say. It was more complicated, however, during Elizabethan times. Players of the time performed so many different roles in so many different plays that it was virtually impossible to keep them all straight. Thus, the prompter's services were frequently required, and the prompter often was blamed if the actors veered too widely from the script. "They are out of their parts sure," says a character in John Fletcher's play *Maid in the Mill*. "It may be 'tis the Book-holder's fault; I'll go see."[45]

Moreover, prompters were often working from barely legible scripts. Few plays of the period were published unless they had already been popular for some time; plays were written to be performed, not read, and there was certainly no market for copies of unknown or unsuccessful dramas. Thus, prompters had longhand copies of the script, many of which were difficult to read. And once the play had been revised a time or two—again by hand—the copy was often downright impossible to follow.

Elizabethan prompters had other responsibilities as well. Like modern stage managers, they kept track of entrances and exits—no small task given the amount of doubling in the plays of the time—and they alerted performers to the need to bring in props or set pieces. To do this, prompters put together a document called a plot, which outlined the sequence of events on the stage. Copies of the plots may have been posted where all actors could see them as they made their entrances and changed their costumes. However, the prompters were the ones who needed the documents the most.

Plots were as simple as they could be without sacrificing accuracy. The prompters could sometimes describe a short scene in a line or two: Scene 20 in a 1585 play called *The Seven Deadly Sins,* for example, is described in a contemporary plot as "Enter Philomele and Tereus. To them Julia [Julia enters and goes to them]."[46] Sometimes, however, the instructions were more elaborate. "Enter Arbactus pursuing Sardanapalus," the same plot explains for Scene 15, "and the ladies fly [run away]. After [that], enter Sarda with as many jewels, robes, and gold as he can carry."[47]

Prompting was a difficult and time-consuming task. Those who filled the roles had to be intensely focused on the action as it unfolded on stage. They had to know the entire outline of each play, and to be able to communicate that knowledge to the other actors. It is not clear whether prompters served exclusively in that role or whether various hired men rotated in and out of the job. Because the work was so difficult, a prompter for any given performance was unlikely to appear on stage that day.

The hired men were a vital part of any Elizabethan acting company. Whether they worked primarily onstage or off, they filled important roles in the troupe. Their ability to portray secondary characters fleshed out the plots of the dramas and added to the story. Their work with costumes and their musical abilities helped the play to look and sound appealing. Without the prompters, the performances could easily have degenerated into chaos. Though the hired men got little credit and attention for their labors, the show could not have gone on without them.

CHAPTER 3

PREPARING A PRODUCTION

The performance of a play in Elizabethan times was the culmination of considerable effort on the part of sharers, apprentices, and hired men. Many hours of difficult, painstaking, and time-consuming work went into the preparations. Not all members of a troupe were involved in every aspect of readying the production for the stage. Still, between choosing, casting, rehearsing, and costuming a play, there was plenty of responsibility for everyone.

CHOOSING PLAYS

At the start of each year, an Elizabethan theater company created a list of plays to present. The sharers made this decision, and they began by deciding which of their earlier productions were worth repeating. Recycling old material had several important advantages. The actors already knew their lines, movements on stage, and en-

trances. Similarly, costumes and sets were available if the play had recently been performed, needing only minor alterations to repair rips or to fit newly hired players.

Another consideration was the potential audience. Shows that had brought in high receipts one year were good candidates to repeat as moneymakers in the future. Thus, plays that had done well financially were often held over and performed again the next year. Lord Strange's Men, for example, performed a play called *The Jew of Malta* during the spring of 1592. It was their top-grossing production, earning an average take of just over two pounds a performance, and they were quick to bring it back again the next year.

But the sharers had to be careful when they decided to revive plays they had already produced. Plays that had been unpopular with audiences one year were unlikely to be any more appealing the next. The same year that they brought back *The Jew of Malta,* for example, Strange's Men also staged a revival of the much less successful *Sir John Mandeville.* Considerations other than money probably drove the decision; historian Neil Carson suggests that "the wishes of the leading actor"[48] may have been the reason. Whatever the cause for the revival, the company could not have been pleased with the audiences drawn by the production. *Sir John Mandeville* was a financial disaster, averaging only eleven shillings a performance.

Moreover, the Elizabethan public was notoriously fickle. Even if a play had been a tremendous hit one year, it could be a flop when the company tried to perform it again a year or two later. Fashions came and went with lightning speed, and what seemed fresh and new one year might seem dull and trite the next. Plays filled with topical references to current events were particularly likely to fade from the public eye, but such a fate could happen to any drama.

Finally, novelty was a virtue as far as the Elizabethans were concerned. While some theatergoers were no doubt delighted to watch the same plays year after year, most audiences demanded something new. A theatrical troupe that did not meet these needs would quickly find itself losing business to its competitors. Thus, while there were distinct advantages to recycling old plays, there were also advantages to preparing something new.

New Plays

As a result, despite the time and the expense incurred by producing a brand-new play, almost half of all dramas presented each year had never been performed before. The need for novelty meant that acting troupes were constantly looking for new material. A few were lucky enough to have a resident playwright, such as William Shakespeare of the Lord Chamberlain's Men, who could turn out a new play more or less on demand. But even Shakespeare could not meet the demand for new plays by himself.

Most theatrical companies, therefore, had to find new scripts wherever they could. Fortunately for them, Elizabethan London was full of poorly paid playwrights who were desperate to have theatrical troupes purchase their work. Better yet, the playwrights worked at lightning speed, so there were always many plays to choose from. The swift pace of completion is suggested by playwright Ben Jonson's dismissal for being "[too] slow an inventor"[49] because it once took him five full weeks to write a play. Given such speed and the number of playwrights, there was a decided buyer's market when it came to scripts.

But if finding a script was easy, finding an appropriate one was not as sim-

❧ PLAYS ❧

Elizabethan plays fit into three broad categories: tragedies, comedies, and histories. Tragedies, like Shakespeare's *Othello* or *Romeo and Juliet,* presented sad stories of treachery, broken hearts, and revenge. It was standard practice for several characters to kill each other or possibly themselves. In some cases, tragedies featured a hero with a personality flaw that ultimately brought about his downfall. In others, the tragedy was not the fault of any one person but of fate—a popular concept in Elizabethan times.

Comedies, in contrast, were lighthearted and often frothy. They featured visual gags, silly mix-ups, and quick verbal wordplay. Some featured serious moments, along with scenes that were exciting or dramatic rather than funny, while others were satirical. But regardless of the dangers and complications, the comedies ended with everything turning out all right—or, as Shakespeare titled one of his comedies, *All's Well That Ends Well.* Shakespeare's *Twelfth Night* is another example of this genre.

Historical plays were also popular with Elizabethan playgoers. These plays dramatized important events and figures of earlier times, generally medieval England or classical Greece and Rome. Among the most famous of these are Shakespeare's *Henry IV,* a two-part work dealing with an early English king, and *Julius Caesar,* which tells of the events surrounding the death of the Roman emperor. Historical plays could be comic, tragic, or include elements of both; but they are generally considered separately from the other two genres.

A movie still depicts the funeral of Juliet in Shakespeare's great tragedy Romeo and Juliet.

ple. Some scripts were too long. Others called for too many characters for most troupes to perform, even with doubling. The Elizabethan plays that survive today are generally considered to be masterpieces of drama, but the truth is that many dramas of the period were dreadful. Historian M.C. Bradbrook writes disparagingly of "the new depths of incoherence"[50] represented by some

Thomas Dekker was one of four scriptwriters hired to pen the play A Late Murder of the Son upon the Mother.

of the worst Elizabethan plays. The sharers frequently would have seen scripts that were dull, poorly written, and far from worthy of performance.

To avoid wasting their time, the bigger troupes often contacted well-known playwrights directly and commissioned works from them. Occasionally—and especially if a new play was needed quickly—the "writer" was not an individual, but a syndicate. In 1624, for instance, Ralph Savage of the Red Bull Company, hired four men to jointly write a play called *A Late Murder of the Son*

upon the Mother. Thomas Dekker, one of the four writers, explained later that his contribution had been "two sheets of paper containing the first act . . . and a speech in the last scene of the last act."[51]

Whether a play had been commissioned or not, the sharers of a troupe arranged to meet with the scriptwriter before buying the work. These meetings usually took place in alehouses, the Elizabethan equivalent of a bar or restaurant. Alehouses were public places, but there was nevertheless an element of privacy to them; as one observer pointed out, the buildings had "partitions between the tables so that one table cannot overlook the next."[52] Thus, shielded from prying eyes—and more importantly, open ears—the playwright would then read his script aloud. Next, the sharers would confer and decide whether the play was right for them.

If the play suited the company, the playwright received a fee of several pounds. No matter how successful the play turned out to be, the writer had no further financial interest in the production. This fact infuriated some playwrights, who felt that the real work was theirs. Writer Robert Greene angrily dismissed actors as mere "puppets . . . that speak from our mouths."[53] But whether Greene and his fellow playwrights liked it or not, there were many more writers in London than there were troupes to perform their plays. Consequently, the actors held the cards.

LICENSING

Once the play had been chosen, the players turned the script over to the government for its approval. This process was called licensing. Elizabeth and the kings who succeeded her were generally supportive of the theater, but they worried that plays could carry antigovernment messages. Texts were closely examined by the government before they could be presented. Often, government officials would eliminate dialogue or change the names of characters if they felt the political satire was too pointed. Sometimes, the rulers evaluated the scripts themselves. "This is too insolent," said King Charles about a line in a play by Philip Massinger, "and [is] to be changed." [54]

Licensing was a frustrating step for the troupes. As a practical matter, it used up precious time that could have been spent learning lines and preparing costumes. It also cost money: During the late 1500s, companies had to pay seven shillings to have a play examined. And it sometimes resulted in changes that threatened the artistic integrity of

◌ PLAYWRIGHTS ◌

The life of a playwright was not an easy one. Elizabethans believed that it was the troupe, not the script, that made the play a success. Londoners went to see the Admiral's Men or the Queen's Company, not to see the latest show by Ben Jonson or Thomas Heywood. As long as a script was decently written and at least moderately exciting, the people of the time agreed, a good company could make it popular. While the troupes worked with certain playwrights more often than they worked with others, it is likely that this appreciation had more to do with the writers' reliability and punctuality in turning in their work than with any sense that they wrote exceptionally brilliant or moving plays.

As a result, most playwrights of the time labored in relative obscurity.

Very little is known about John Ford, for example, or John Lyly, both of whom had several important plays performed. For that matter, many question marks surround the life of Shakespeare. And most of the playwrights about whom something is known led rather dismal lives. Robert Greene deserted a wife and child and died young, probably from venereal disease. Jonson was hotheaded and offended almost everyone he knew. Christopher Marlowe, nearly as quarrelsome as Jonson, was killed in a barroom fight at the age of twenty-nine. Thomas Dekker, prolific but perpetually broke, went to prison for debt on many occasions. Their stories were repeated by many other playwrights of the time.

the work. If censors deemed a line or an entire scene unacceptable, then they simply crossed out the offending passage; it was up to the company to rewrite the sections so the story still made sense.

Worse yet, the careful government scrutiny directly impacted the troupes' ability to make money. Political satire was quite popular with Elizabethan audiences, and plays indulging in humor at the government's expense were often very successful. In 1624, for instance, one troupe presented a play called *Game at Chess,* which made veiled references to the king of Spain and other well-known persons. The play was the company's most successful by far, and troupes longed for greater freedom to engage in political satire.

However, licensing was absolutely necessary. An actor who appeared in a performance of an unlicensed play was committing a serious offense. Indeed, it was even a crime to add extra material to the play after the licensing had been completed. During times of political instability companies had to be especially careful. In 1597, for example, officials noted that the Lord Admiral's Men had presented a play, Ben Jonson's *Isle of Dogs,* which "contain[ed] very seditious and slanderous matter."[55] The penalties were steep: Officials jailed Jonson as well as the lead actors Robert Shaa and Gabriel Spencer.

EDITING, SCRIPTS, AND SIDES

After licensing, the sharers and prompters worked together to edit and annotate the script. The prompters marked in stage directions and other information pertaining to sets or special effects. "Gascoine and Hubert below: ready to open the trap door for Mr. Taylor,"[56] read one such mark on a contemporary script of Philip Massinger's *Believe as You List.* They also created the plot, the outline of the script that detailed the characters' entrances, exits, and costume changes.

The prompters and lead actors often made a few extra edits to the play after licensing. The law required no additions, but cutting could still be done—and often was. If a scene or a line did not appear to be effective, it was excised at this stage. Cuts were also made due to length; ideally, plays would run no longer than two hours or so. Because few working manuscripts survive from the time, it is difficult to tell today how prevalent editing was. But existing scripts generally show several changes made during this part of preparation.

The next step was to make a clean copy of the script, along with annotations, for the prompter's use. Making copies during Elizabethan times was a complicated process. Printing was extremely expensive and out of the question for small orders, so copies had to be handmade. Unfortunately, copying by hand often led to inaccuracies. It was also slow and cumbersome. The prompters worked with copyists hired for the occasion to produce a single clean copy of the script. Depending on the length of the play and the number of copyists at work, the process could take as much as two weeks.

Actors needed scripts, too, but time and budget did not permit a full copy for each man. Instead, actors received what were known as "sides." A side was a rolled sheet of parchment on which were written all the lines spoken by the player, together with his entrances and exits. Each man had his own side, prepared by the prompter or by professional copyists. The sides were barely sufficient. They did not give players a sense of how much time passed between each speech; indeed, if cues were given at all, they were rarely more than a word or two. Then again, it was probably not within the resources of most companies to do more. Certainly the sides, flawed as they were, proved better than nothing.

CASTING

While the final revisions were being made, the troupe's sharers were also casting the play. As far as can be determined today, casting was a group effort; no one person was solely in charge of assigning parts. Certain well-respected members of companies may have had more say in casting decisions than others; but for the most part, the sharers decided together how to divide the roles among the actors.

Today, the process of casting takes up a great deal of a theater company's time. In Elizabethan England, however, the procedure was far simpler. The troupes were so-called repertory companies, in which the actors for each play were drawn exclusively from the members of the company. There was no need to hold casting calls outside the troupe. Even if a rival company had an actor who would have been wonderful in a certain role, the group made do with the men they already had.

Casting revivals was especially easy. Unless there had been significant changes in the composition of the troupe since the last time the play had been presented, the sharers could simply repeat earlier cast lists—and most did exactly that. But casting new plays did not usually present a problem. Many of these works were written with a particular company in mind, so the playwright created characters that would fit the physical attributes and acting capabilities of the men who belonged to the troupe.

Moreover, most of the leading actors of the time specialized in certain kinds of roles. Richard Tarlton, for example, was known for what one contemporary called his "wonderful plentiful pleasant extemporal [improvised] wit."[57] That sense of humor often got him cast as the comedic lead in the

The great Elizabethan actor Edward Alleyn was highly regarded for his work in tragedies and historical plays.

plays his troupe presented. Edward Alleyn, on the other hand, was considered better suited for serious roles, such as in tragedies or historical plays. As one writer put it, he "made any part (especially a majestic one) to become

him."[58] And Stephen Hammerton won his fame for portraying young romantic heroes. The sharers would have been aware of the strengths and weaknesses of each actor, and it is likely that there was general agreement as to which parts the various players should have.

On occasion, actors were cast in roles that may not have best suited them. The comic actor Thomas Pope, for example, played at least one serious character—the general Arbactus in a play called *The Seven Deadly Sins*. Will Kempe, another famous comedian, was assigned the minor role of the Nurse's servant Peter when the Chamberlain's Men put on *Romeo and Juliet*. And Anthony Turner, though a well-respected sharer, played the small role of a kitchen servant in a play called *The Fair Maid of the West*.

It is not entirely clear why such unusual casting decisions were made. They may have been designed to stretch the talents of a company's leading actors. Pope's troupe was surely better off if he could play occasional serious roles in addition to serving as the company's comedian. Likewise, since companies performed a grueling schedule of plays, sharers may have been assigned small roles as a way of giving them an occasional rest. There was another possibility, too. As Marchette Chute suggests in the case of Kempe, "The company as a whole evidently felt that Kempe could be used to best advantage in a small role, and [so] that was the one he played."[59]

TIME

The process of choosing, copying, editing, licensing, and casting a play often took several weeks, with the licensing and copying phases being the most time-consuming. But companies did their best to hurry the procedure along. Two weeks between choosing a play and starting rehearsals seems to have been the standard that most troupes tried to meet. No doubt this goal often meant cutting corners, especially where the copying of parts was concerned.

In a few cases, though, even two weeks struck the members of a troupe as excessive. For a play called *Fortunatus,* one company cut the time span to six days, and another group of actors allowed only three days to elapse between deciding to perform a new play called *Jephtha* and the start of rehearsals. The Admiral's Men actually started rehearsing *Two Angry Women* in 1599 before the writing of the play had been completed. Exactly why the

Although an acclaimed comic actor, Will Kempe (pictured) was assigned a small role in the tragedy Romeo and Juliet.

companies felt such need for haste is unknown. As historian Neil Carson explained, the pace indicates that "the attention to detail we expect in contemporary productions was almost certainly impossible"[60] for the Elizabethans. It is probable that many of the finished productions were rough indeed.

That was particularly true because some of the actors knew nothing about a new play before rehearsals began. Shakespeare's *A Midsummer Night's Dream* includes a scene in which Peter Quince, an amateur actor, hands out parts for a play called *Pyramus and Thisby.* None of the company members have any idea who the characters are. "You must take Thisby on you," says Quince to a member of the troupe named Francis Flute, who replies, "What is Thisby? A wandering knight?" Quince, in turn, explains, "It is the lady that Pyramus must love."[61] Shakespeare may well have exaggerated the process for comic effect, but it is likely that the basic outline is accurate.

A contemporary stage production of Shakespeare's The Tempest *features the simple stage set common in Elizabethan times.*

❧ THE DEVELOPMENT OF THEATERS ❧

In the early days of Queen Elizabeth I's reign, theatrical troupes usually played in the homes of the noblemen who sponsored them. When the actors' talents were not required, they often got permission to play at inns, which in those days were large U-shaped buildings built around an open court. The troupes set up informal stages inside the court, charged admission, and divided the proceeds with the innkeeper. For the most part, companies would give only two or three performances at an inn and then move on to another establishment in a different section of the city, though longer runs of popular plays were possible.

As Elizabeth's rule continued, though, that situation changed. Greater independence from lordly sponsors meant that fewer plays were presented to nobility alone. At the inns, meanwhile, the runs became longer and the stages more elaborate. By the early 1570s, the Bull, the Bel Savage, and the Cross Keys, along with several other London inns, had become better known for their theatrical presentations than for the food and lodging they offered. "Where shall we go?" asked a lesson from a phrase book intended for Italian visitors to England, as quoted in Wickham, Berry, and Ingram, *English Professional Theatre, 1530–1660.* "To a play at the Bull, or else to some other place."

But the inns did not keep their status for long. By the end of Elizabeth's reign, plays were performed mostly in theaters built expressly for the purpose of presenting dramas. The first of these new playhouses, known simply as The Theatre, was completed in 1577. The notion caught on, and before long, there were many others, such as the Curtain, the Rose, the Globe (manufactured from pieces of The Theatre after it was pulled down in 1598), the Swan, and Blackfriars—which was indoors and considered a cut above the others. The age of the English public theater had dawned.

While the sharers made the plays ready for rehearsals, hired men prepared the necessary costumes, sets, and props. Fortunately for the company, many individual items would have been on hand from earlier shows. That was even true for new productions. Sets, in particular, tended to be minimal: "books lying confusedly within the curtain"[62] was generally enough description to indicate that a scene took place in a study or library. Moreover, props and set pieces such as goblets, tables, tombs, and swords were standard equipment for most Elizabethan dramas, and a king in one play could wear the same robes as a king in another.

However, just as costumes wore out or needed alterations, it was sometimes necessary to construct new props or replace battered set pieces. A few plays called for elaborate outfits or special scenery not likely to have been used in earlier shows. Items such as trees with golden apples, mentioned in the play *Fortunatus,* would have been less readily available than thrones or cauldrons. No matter how slapdash the work, creating these new pieces took time. The earlier the hired men began the process, the sooner the play could be presented.

REHEARSALS

Rehearsals were the final step in preparing a production. Companies typically spent mornings rehearsing one or more of the plays in their repertory. They started early in the day because they performed in the afternoon, and they needed time to get into costume and make the stage ready for the paying customers. Having to rehearse and perform on the same day made for a very tiring experience for the actors.

Perhaps as a result, Elizabethan companies tried to get away with as few rehearsals as possible. One historian has argued that no new play ever received more than ten rehearsals before its first performance—an extremely low number in comparison to standard practice today. However, the actors in most companies had worked together often and needed little time to get to know each other's capabilities. The plays of the pe-

riod, moreover, tended to follow similar structures and sequences, which also made the job of rehearsing somewhat easier.

And actors, too, were expected to learn their lines mainly on their own. As Peter Quince exhorts his fellow actors in the *Midsummer Night's Dream* play within a play, "Here are your parts; and I am to entreat you, request you, and desire you, to con [know] them by to-morrow night."[63] Ideally, professional players of the time were supposed to have their parts more or less memorized soon after the start of rehearsals. It is hard to believe that they always did—or even that they all managed to learn their lines during the rehearsal period. Indeed, the low number of rehearsals suggests again that Elizabethan companies preferred speed to quality: It was better to get a less-than-perfect play on stage in a short time than to delay the production until all the kinks had been worked through.

But rehearsals were nevertheless important. It would have been foolhardy for a troupe to go onstage without having run through the play at least a few times. Entrances, costumes, and lines often needed adjusting, and the only way to know for certain was to try them out. Attendance at rehearsals was therefore mandatory. Player Robert Dawes, for example, signed a contract promising to "attend all such rehearsal[s] which shall the night before the rehearsal be given publicly out [announced]."[64] The penalty for tardiness was set by his contract at a fine of twelve pence. For missing the rehearsal altogether, Dawes would have been charged two shillings.

It is not clear who ran the rehearsals. Plays of the Elizabethan period do not seem to have had directors in the modern sense. On the other hand, it is unlikely that every actor decided all or even most aspects of costume, blocking, and characterization for himself. Some historians have suggested that the most experienced sharers took turns serving as a sort of actor-in-charge. Others argue that the task

would more likely have fallen to sharers filling the roles of minor actors, since they would have had more time to spend looking over the production as a whole.

Playwrights, in some cases, are another possibility. There is evidence that Ben Jonson directed some of his own works, and speculation that Shakespeare did the same. Still, handing the direction over to the playwrights was not standard procedure. Most writers paid little attention to their works once they had sold the scripts. "I see not mine own plays,"[65] reported author George Chapman.

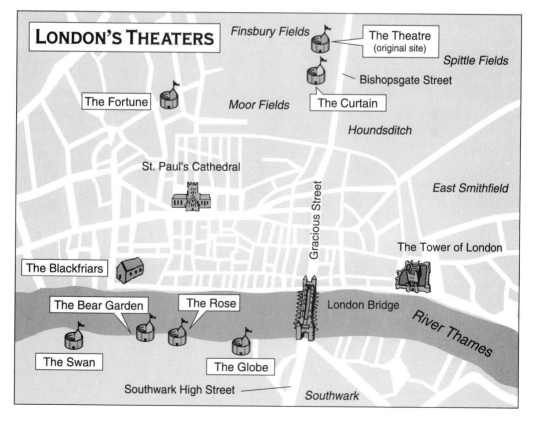

SCHEDULING AND ADVERTISING

Once rehearsals were under way, only the scheduling and advertising of the show remained. The first part was straightforward, because Elizabethan theater companies had no set schedule. Each afternoon, the sharers simply presented whichever play they thought would draw the biggest audience. There was no weekly or monthly pattern to the performances, nor any sense that a particular show ought to be repeated day after day until audiences tired of it. Thus, it was easy to insert a new play anywhere in the schedule. Unfamiliar plays ordinarily attracted large audiences, at least at first, so sharers were inclined to open new shows on days that otherwise would not have attracted much business.

The final step was to advertise. In the last days before the production opened, hired men and sharers combed the city putting up playbills to call attention to the performances. The playbills were printed sheets, expensive for the company but nevertheless important if the troupe wished to draw any kind of audience. One example survives today, which describes the scenes of the play in flowery and dramatic language; it was probably typical of the playbills of the time.

After the advertising was complete and the rehearsals were finished, the preparations were over. The performance was all that remained.

CHAPTER 4

THE PERFORMANCE

Performing a play was a difficult task for an Elizabethan troupe. Actors sweated in heavy and uncomfortable costumes and strained their voices to be heard above the audience. The physical efforts of sword fighting, dancing, and tumbling exhausted the players—men and boys alike—especially since they had usually completed a rehearsal for another play only an hour or two earlier. And the mental stress of speaking lines, making costume changes, and carrying out their blocking wearied the actors even further. Nor was there any guarantee that the audience would like what it saw.

Still, the performance was the reason for all the hard work that had gone before. Although being onstage could be tiring and anxiety-provoking, the purpose of being an actor was to appear in front of an audience. The members of the troupe looked forward with eagerness and anticipation to each perform-

ance. They knew that there was no greater reward than the applause they received at the end of a good show, and no greater excitement than speaking from the stage while hundreds of audience members strained to catch every word.

THE START OF THE SHOW

Most Elizabethan performances began at about two o'clock in the afternoon, although some sources suggest that plays occasionally started in the late morning. The shows had a standard running time of approximately two hours, although a few dragged on longer. Especially in the wintertime, the approaching darkness made it necessary to wrap things up as speedily as possible. In 1594, in fact, the Lord Chamberlain assured London officials that his players would "have done [with their performances] between four and five." [66]

Performances of the time did not follow most modern conventions. Today, for example, the dimming of the house lights in the theater generally signals the start of a performance. But that was not possible in Elizabethan times. Most playhouses were open-air and all, of course, predated electricity. While candles or torches were used to help illuminate the stage under certain circumstances, theaters of the time lacked artificial light. In place of dimmed lights, three quick blasts on a trumpet, played by one of the hired men, alerted the audience that the actors were ready to begin.

Another important difference involved the beginning of the action.

Open-air theaters were common during the Elizabethan era. Plays often began at midday to take advantage of natural light.

Most modern theaters have curtains at the front of the stage, which members of the stage crew open when the show is about to begin. Although Elizabethan theaters occasionally had hangings on the walls, the concept of shielding the stage from the audience was unknown. Instead of opening the curtain to reveal the actors behind it, Elizabethan troupes stayed off the stage as the audience got ready for the opening of the show. Then, the actors taking part in the first scene simply walked onto the stage and began speaking their lines.

Some plays, however, offered the audience a brief introduction before starting the action. Many Elizabethan dramas began with short prologues. Usually delivered by one of the leading actors, these speeches served several purposes. One was thoroughly pragmatic: The prologue was a final alert to audience members who had not yet focused their attention on the stage. Playwrights and actors also sometimes sprinkled the prologue with references to the entertainment value of the upcoming play or stated their wish that the audience enjoy the show. "Now, luck yet send us, and a little wit,"[67] begins a typical example from the prologue to Ben Jonson's *Volpone.*

The prologues had one other important use, as well. Frequently, they described the plot in a few short lines. The prologue of *Volpone,* for example, begins with the words:

Volpone, childless, rich, feigns sick, despairs,

Offers his state [estate] to hopes of several heirs.[68]

Speeches such as this were the equivalent of a television show summary today: They simply alerted the audience to watch for some of the people and situations they would see during the afternoon. In a few cases, the prologues completely gave away the play's ending. The opening speech to *Romeo and Juliet,* for example, deftly explains that the show deals with a bitter feud between two wealthy families—and then informs audience members that they soon will see "a pair of star-crossed lovers take their life."[69]

While these prologues certainly took away from the show's suspense, the Elizabethans were not terribly concerned with the loss. Most Elizabethan dramas were not original. *Romeo and Juliet,* for example, was adapted from a long narrative poem published in 1562, which in turn stemmed from much older sources; it would have been a familiar tale to theatergoers of Shakespeare's time. Audience members were more interested in seeing how the tale would be performed rather than in finding out what would happen next.

From the actors' standpoint, the main goal of the prologue was to whet the audience's appetite for the show. That meant beginning the play with a bang. Telling playgoers that they soon would witness the suicides of two young lovers was designed to draw them into the action; and given the popularity of *Romeo and Juliet,* the strategy seems to have been successful. Certainly, a bored and restless audience could make the show a financial disaster for those who performed it. It was better to start with a punchy, clever speech that left the audience eager to see more, even if it did destroy some of the suspense.

SCENERY AND THE IMAGINATION

The settings of Elizabethan plays were limited only by the imaginations of the playwrights. The dramas of the time usually took place in a variety of locations, both indoors and out, and the scene shifted frequently. *The Duchess of Malfi,* for example, has scenes that take place in "A Gallery in the Duchess's Palace"; "A Room in the Cardinal's Palace at Rome"; and "A Public Place in Milan,"[70] among others. Other plays call for scenes in forests, huts, deserts, cemeteries, and caves.

But by modern standards, the stages were curiously empty of set pieces, backdrops, and other indications of where the scenes took place. Elizabethan companies did not paint and hang backdrops to show the settings of each play, as would be common practice today. The stage, indeed, would look little different from one scene to the next. Some historians argue that

Elizabethan troupes used placards or announcers to inform the audience of the setting for the next scene. However, most agree that players and audience members were usually expected to use their imaginations.

They did have some help. Playwrights often inserted dialogue at the beginning of scenes to establish where the characters were, especially if the new scene was in a markedly different place from the previous one. "Walk the horses down the hill,"[71] Lord Lovell commands his servants at the beginning of Act 3 of Massinger's *A New Way to Pay Old Debts.* Lovell's order helps to move the plot ahead; he wants the servants to leave so he can speak to another character in private. But more importantly, the command alerts the audience to the rural, outdoor setting of the scene.

PROPS AND SET PIECES

The use of props could also make it easier for audiences to orient themselves. One scene of Thomas Heywood's *A Woman Killed with Kindness,* for example, begins with the entrance of several servants. According to the stage directions, one man is carrying "a wooden knife; . . . another the salt and bread; another the table-cloth and napkins."[72] No dialogue was necessary to tell Elizabethan audiences that the scene involved a banquet. The entrance of hired men carrying torches, similarly, might indicate that darkness had fallen. Costumes, too, could serve as a kind of

A modern staging of Romeo and Juliet *leaves much to the audience's imagination, as did performances during the Elizabethan period.*

theatrical shorthand. Dressing an actor in hunting regalia, for example, was a signal that the next scene would take place outdoors, while a nightshirt would indicate a bedchamber.

Elizabethan companies occasionally used set pieces to help create the setting. An inventory of the items owned by the Lord Admiral's Men in 1599, for example, included "3 trees, 3 rocks . . . 3 tombs, 2 frames, [and] 2 steeples,"[73] along with a bedstead, a cage, and a

piece intended to represent a stable. Each of these items, placed carefully on the stage, could give a clue to the surroundings. The presence of a throne would naturally indicate a royal court, while an imitation bush set at the edge of the stage would suggest an outdoor setting.

But most of these set pieces were integral parts of the action. An actor might hide behind a bush, fall asleep on a rock, or discover the tomb of his beloved. These set pieces were there to be used, not simply to decorate the stage or to hint at a certain place for the upcoming scene. Theater companies limited their use of set pieces partly because they cost money and took time to construct. Moreover, setting them up wasted time and manpower. Audiences did not wish to wait while minor characters, still in costume, hauled out elaborate pieces of scenery for a scene that might last only two or three minutes.

THE STAGE

Relatively little is known about the stages on which Elizabethan actors performed. Evidence from drawings, accounts, and stage directions, however, indicates that most stages of the period shared at least a few features. Perhaps most noticeably, the stage was nearer to the audience than it is today. Some au-dience members actually sat on one side of the stage, and the stage itself jutted out directly into the crowded gallery. When the house was full, playgoers surrounded the actors on three sides. Thus, the action melted into the crowd in a way that is uncommon today.

Most stages had a raised area in the back, too, a sort of ministage that could be used as a house's second story, the deck of a ship, or the top of a city wall. In *Romeo and Juliet,* Juliet would have appeared on this part of the stage during the famous balcony scene. Many theaters probably had another small space in the back that was even with the floor to be used as a tomb, cave, or closet. These extra spaces allowed the players more freedom and variety in staging scenes.

❧ STAGING AND SIR PHILIP SIDNEY ❧

A few Elizabethan audience members complained bitterly about the relatively bare stages. One of these was Sir Philip Sidney, a nobleman who summed up his confusion over the conventions of staging in these words, quoted in Marchette Chute, Shakespeare of London*:*

You shall have Asia on the one side [of the stage] and Affrick [Africa] on the other, and so many underkingdoms that the player, when he cometh on, must ever begin with telling where he is, or else the tale will not be conceived [understood]. Now we shall have three ladies walk to gather flowers, and then we must believe the stage to be a garden. By and by we hear news of shipwreck in the same place, and then we are to blame if we accept it not for a rock.

But Sidney was an exception. Most audience members embraced the conventions. They were able to use their imaginations to transport themselves to whatever location the play demanded.

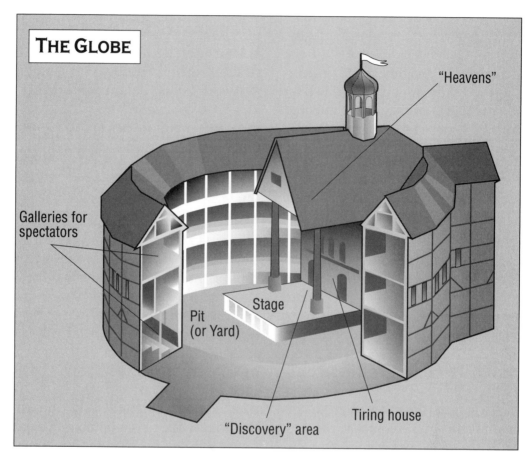

THE GLOBE

"Heavens"

Galleries for spectators

Stage

Pit (or Yard)

"Discovery" area

Tiring house

Even though the audience pressed up against the stage in most directions, the stages of the time nevertheless had two doors from which an actor could make entrances and exits. Both were probably on the back wall of the stage, one on the right and the other on the left. As a stage direction from *The Duchess of Malfi* reads, "Exeunt [exit] Duchess and Ladies. Exit, on the other side, Bosola."[74] The exits took the players to an area backstage where the costumes and set pieces were stored, and where they could quickly change

their costumes if that was necessary. Given the numbers of parts most actors were expected to play, it usually was. Many actors of the time spent a great deal of the production traveling between these dressing rooms and the stage.

COSTUMES AND SPECIAL EFFECTS

Although their sets and scenery tended to be minimal, Elizabethan theater troupes did not stint when it came to costumes. Costumes were both fancy and costly, attractive to the audience although bulky and uncomfortable for the wearers. One inventory of items from a company of the time is full of references to "satin doublets" and "velvet gowns," many of them "embroidered with silk" or "laid with gold lace."[75] The splendor of the costumes often made the stage appear to be hosting an Elizabethan fashion show rather than a play. The troupes vied with each other to offer the best and most striking costumes.

Nor did the troupes ignore special effects. Most stages, for example, were equipped with trapdoors. These were especially useful for plays in which the devil made a sudden appearance. But they could also be used as exits for characters condemned to eternal damnation or serve as entrances for actors creeping out of caves and underground chambers. To operate the trapdoors smoothly, companies stationed a hired man or two beneath the stage. The use of the trapdoor created a little extra variety for the performance, thus sharpening the interest of the audience—and increasing the likelihood that the play would be a success.

Actors also could be "flown" onto the stage. For this effect, hired men helped the players into harnesses as they prepared to make their entrances. Then they used mechanical equipment, similar to small modern-day cranes, to pick the actors up and swing them into the view of the audience.

These contraptions also transported set pieces, occasionally together with the actors. "Exit Venus," reads a typical stage direction from a play called *Alphonsus*, "or if you can conveniently, let a chair come down from the top of the stage and draw her up."[76] Again, these entrances added spice and dramatic interest to the production.

SWORD FIGHTS AND MURDERS

Likewise, many performances—especially histories and tragedies—involved battle scenes, duels, and other assorted atrocities in which characters were injured or killed. Audiences looked forward with great anticipation to these sequences. As historian Ivor Brown explains, "The spectators relished the sight of a mutilated body and a stage piled high with corpses."[77] The troupes did not need to string up ocean backdrops and build ornate throne rooms on the stage to entertain their audiences, but skimping on battles and blood was a sure way to bankruptcy.

The stage directions for the battles, duels, and murders are generally scanty. During one such scene in *Macbeth*, Shakespeare simply writes, "Enter fighting, and Macbeth slain."[78] Another, in *Romeo and Juliet*, is only a little more specific: In one copy of the play, a direction calls for one character to stab another "under Romeo's arm"[79] as Romeo attempts to stop the fight. Despite the lack of obvious direction, there is little doubt

❧ SETS, PROPS, AND COSTUMES ❧

It is not entirely clear why costumes were so important to Elizabethan players and audiences while sets and props were largely ignored. Part of the reason may have been practical: A costume could be changed offstage while the action continued, whereas replacing sets or backdrops would have interrupted the flow of the play. And part may have involved artistic considerations. Actors may have looked forward to the challenge of setting the mood without much help from the stage and its properties. While costumes did help to establish the scene, they were of limited use—especially since all actors wore standard Elizabethan dress, regardless of their characters' ethnicity or historical period.

The real reason for the importance of costumes probably lies in the extreme fashion consciousness of Elizabethan England. The wealthy of the period took great pains to dress in fine and elaborate clothing, and the middle class did its best to emulate them. Queen Elizabeth owned three thousand dresses, most given to her by admirers who hoped to win her favor. Fancy fabrics and designs were popular, and no lady or gentleman dared to be seen in public without the latest outfit or accessory. Theatergoers may have demanded authenticity in costume simply because finery was such an important part of their world.

Queen Elizabeth's interest in fashion influenced costume design in the theater.

In the 1968 film, Romeo and Juliet, *one character stabs another under Romeo's arm. Here, as in the Elizabethan theater, swordplay is colorfully staged.*

that the sword-fighting scenes were well choreographed. Audiences of the time were knowledgeable about fencing and its moves, and historians agree that acting troupes gave the playgoers what they wanted.

The troupes did the same when it came to deaths. Actors whose characters were about to be killed would fill small containers with animal blood and pop them open at the appropriate moment.

Nor did Elizabethan troupes stop with blood. In *The Battle of Alacazar,* a character was disemboweled on stage, an action that required the company to obtain not only the blood but also the liver, lungs, and heart of a sheep. Presumably, the organs were obtained fresh for each performance.

Human body parts were also a common feature of Elizabethan plays. Shakespeare's *Titus Andronicus* has a scene in which a character's hand is chopped off; a stage direction just before the end of Macbeth reads, "Enter Macduff, with Macbeth's head." [80] Human heads and hands were a little harder to come by than sheep's blood, but the actors were equal to the challenge. They used clay, cloth, and other materials to fashion substitutes that would "read," or look real from the audience. Every company would have had what one actor called "legs and arms of men (well and lively wrought) to be let fall in numbers on the ground, as bloody as might be." [81]

Still, it was up to the players to make the scenes look real. Actors had to be competent swordsmen to excite and impress the audience. If two fencers were parrying and thrusting without real energy, or if their moves were awkward and poorly rehearsed, the audience would notice—and jeer them loudly. Nor could it have been easy to handle the sheep organs or the faked limbs well enough to make the action believable. Doing so, though, could make the difference between creating a moving, intensely dramatic scene and one that read like a parody of itself.

ACTING CONVENTIONS

The plays of Elizabethan times were usually divided into five acts of two or more scenes each. The acts were not necessarily of equal length. Neither were the scenes; the first scene of Shakespeare's *Macbeth,* for example, is only 12 lines long, while the last scene of the fourth act runs 242 lines. Theater groups today would commonly add one or two intermissions between the acts, to give audiences a chance to stretch and players a moment to rest. Elizabethan companies may or may not have done the same, but most evidence suggests that they usually did not.

If there were no intermissions, it is easy to imagine that the players would have been exhausted by the end of the show. But even if there were intermissions, the day was still tiring. Players performed in the open air, regardless of the weather; they had to project their voices over the noise of the crowd; they had to perform in heavy and uncomfortable costumes. Moreover, they usually had been rehearsing and doing other tasks for much of the morning, and they were performing one of a dozen or more plays they were expected to know by heart. Performance was a difficult task.

Just as there were a few shortcuts for setting the stage, there were also some important ways in which players of the time could conserve their energy. One was the Elizabethan conception of character. Most evidence suggests that the actors did not generally see each character as a distinct individual, but rather saw the parts they played as types. Actors probably did not take pains, then, to distinguish between tragic heroes such as Brutus, Macbeth, and King Lear. In their minds, the whole category of parts was more or less interchangeable. That attitude certainly helped to make playing a variety of roles somewhat easier.

Likewise, actors had certain stage conventions for expressing emotions. "To wring the hands is a natural expression of excessive grief," instructed a manual from King Charles's reign. Similarly, "To clasp the right fist often on the left palm is a natural expression used by those who mock, chide, brawl, and insult."[82] Modern audiences expect real or artfully feigned emotion from their actors, but the Elizabethans were often content to look for these and other signals from the stage to let them know how the characters were supposed to be feeling. The better actors probably relied less on such shortcuts than did their more mediocre counterparts, but the convention nevertheless allowed all players to put a little less energy into their performances.

A painting shows King Lear (right) mourning the death of his daughter Cordelia. Elizabethan actors did not particularly differentiate roles such as Lear from other tragic characters, making it less difficult for them to play a variety of parts.

THE AUDIENCE

Because their structures were made of wood, no Elizabethan theater survives today, but contemporary drawings, descriptions, and archeological evidence make it possible to guess at its size and shape. There were several types of seating. Many audience members sat in the gallery, which was a series of benches facing the stage. Most of the seats were under cover, and playgoers paid two or three pennies for them. Most of the other onlookers, poorer or more willing to put up with uncomfortable conditions, paid a penny to stand in the unroofed section of the building. These audience members were commonly known as "groundlings."

The theaters also had a few seats for wealthier patrons. As in modern sports stadiums or opera houses, audience members could pay extra for their own boxes—comfortable seats set off from the rest of the crowd. In some theaters, one or two of these were kept on perpetual standby for lords who might attend a performance. A few audience members, too, notably young men of leisure, paid to sit on stools that were actually on the stage.

By modern standards, the playhouses were small, cramped, and dirty. A Dutch visitor reported that the Swan "accommodates in its seats three thousand persons,"[83] which it did only by sliding people as close together as possible. One historian estimates that an audience member in the gallery of a typical Elizabethan theater was wedged into a space measuring about two feet by two feet—uncomfortable by almost any definition. The groundlings had it even worse. When the theater was full, it is doubtful that they had much more than a square foot of floor space to stand on.

By modern standards, Elizabethan theaters were loud and chaotic. Strolling vendors sold the playgoers food and drinks, which they consumed during the performances, and people moved around as much as the crowded conditions allowed. "The audience's mood," sums up M.C. Bradbrook, "was one of pastime."[84] Playgoers arrived in a mood to be entertained. Thus, if a play did not attract the customers' attention, they would not suffer through it politely and quietly as a modern audience might. Instead, they would ignore the action on stage and talk loudly among themselves instead.

Alternatively, they would heckle the players. This behavior seems to have been especially common among the young men who sat on the stage itself. These men, wrote playwright Thomas Dekker, would "mew at passionate speeches and blare at merry; find fault with the music . . . and whistle at the songs."[85] Occasionally members of the crowd threw rotten fruit at the actors, too. The players sometimes soldiered on with the play, but more often they departed from the script to talk back to the hecklers. Contemporary sources reported that Richard Tarlton, for example,

❧ COURT PERFORMANCES ☙

Once in a while, a company would be summoned to give a theatrical performance at the royal court. Being invited to perform for the monarch was considered a great honor. It was also a wonderful opportunity to make money, since the nobility paid the players handsomely; usually the fee was about ten pounds, or a good deal more than the troupe would make from their regular afternoon performances. And the glory earned the players bragging rights. They could advertise that they had performed for royalty, thus making their own productions more appealing to the masses.

Unfortunately, playing for the nobility was a complicated and wearying task. The players had to ensure that all their sets, instruments, and costumes were in the best condition possible. It would never do for an actor to appear before the queen in a dirty, ragged outfit, or holding a stage prop that had been constructed five years earlier. The actors also needed to be absolutely certain that nothing in their script would offend the royal listeners. Even casual references to the political scene were usually excised, just in case the audience might be insulted.

Finally, the performances at court were in addition to the company's regular schedule, not instead of it. Generally, these performances began late—ten or even eleven o'clock in the evening—and did not end until after midnight. The next day, the players would have to rehearse, retrieve their supplies, and perform their regularly scheduled production, all without falling asleep on their feet. It could not have been easy, but the advantages of court performances made the difficulties worthwhile.

was adept at hurling improvised insults of his own at abusive audience members, should the occasion demand it.

Although the audience could quickly turn against the actors if the play was bad, nothing was more appealing than playing to an enthusiastic crowd of Elizabethans. One contemporary observer noted how eagerly the playgoers could respond to the action on stage. For tragedies, he remarked, it was common to see members of the audiences "weeping and mourning" along with the actors; for comedies, audience members "generally take up a wonderful laughter, and shout together with one voice."[86] A good play and an appreciative audience brought out the best in the playgoers—and no doubt in the actors as well.

CHAPTER 5

ON TOUR

London was the largest, richest, and most cultured city in England during the Elizabethan period. Not surprisingly, most famous and successful theatrical companies of the time were based in London and gave most of their performances there. Troupes such as the Admiral's Men and the King's Men dominated London drama for many years.

But not all of the acting troupes of the time were London companies. At least two hundred troupes, and probably many more, spent their time traveling throughout the rest of England. Little is known about most of these so-called provincial companies, partly because they tended to be small and short-lived, and partly because the most detailed records concern the London troupes. However, these touring players performed for audiences in villages, towns, and smaller cities throughout England;

and a few toured continental Europe as well.

In all likelihood, the provincial companies did not approach the quality or depth of the London companies. Yet, talented actors and troupes often played in the provinces, because the best London companies made tours of their own as well. Every major theatrical troupe of the time took at least one extended journey out of the capital city. Through the years of their existence, in fact, most made several tours.

Traveling—or, as playwright Thomas Dekker described it, "trot[ting] from town to town upon the hard hoof"[87]— brought its own distinctive set of problems. It could also have several important advantages. Regardless of whether touring was a positive or negative experience, it was a fact of life for nearly all Elizabethan actors. And whether an actor toured full-time or only occasionally, he found that life in a traveling

❧ PLAYERS IN EUROPE ❧

While most touring players stayed in England, a few went to continental Europe, where they were very well received. English theater was appealing to the citizens of Italy, France, Sweden, and Germany, among other countries, even if the audience did not speak English. According to this recollection from an Englishman that is quoted in Elizabethan-Jacobean Drama:

Some of our . . . stageplayers came out of England into Germany, and played at Frankfort . . . having neither a complete number of actors nor any good apparel, nor any ornament of the stage, yet the Germans, not understanding a word they said, both men and women, flocked wonderfully to see their gesture and action, rather than hearing them speaking English which they understood not, and pronouncing pieces and patches of English plays, which myself and some Englishmen there present could not hear without great wearisomeness.

The players in this production included Robert Browne of the Admiral's Men, along with several other important actors of the time. But similar crowds also came to see lesser performers—just as long as they were English.

troupe was very different from life in a more settled company.

GOING ON TOUR

Theatrical companies had many reasons for going on tour. Perhaps the most important reason involved the law of supply and demand. Even in England's biggest city, there simply were not enough prospective playgoers to support more than a handful of troupes. Indeed, by most estimates, there were usually no more than five or six companies performing in London at any given time.

Part of the problem was that London's population at the end of the sixteenth century was, by modern standards, quite small. The total number of Londoners probably did not exceed two hundred thousand—and may well not have been even that high. Furthermore, that population included many people who never went to see plays. Puritans and those in sympathy with them scorned plays for religious reasons. Some people were too sick, old, or weak to make the trip. Others were hard at work during the times when troupes presented their plays or simply lacked any interest in dramatic entertainment. Still others were too poor to afford even the cheapest admission. Of those who did go, most went only occasionally.

Since the audience for London plays was limited, it did not make economic sense for dozens of companies to set up shop in the city. Most would have gone bankrupt—and very quickly at that. As a result, many companies—especially those with less money and less talented or well-known actors—chose instead to take their skills on the road. For many of these groups, becoming a touring company was the right move: By leaving London, they avoided direct competition with the bigger, wealthier, and better-known troupes.

Moreover, the touring companies found a ready-made and often enthusiastic audience in the provinces. The men and women who lived in England's smaller communities may have been less sophisticated than their London counterparts, but they enjoyed a good play by Shakespeare, Dekker, or Christopher Marlowe as much as anyone. In a time without film, sound recording, or good roads for transportation, the arrival of a theater company was the only chance most provincial Englanders had to see a real stage show. For many troupes, the opportunity to tap this market was a very good reason to go on the road.

COMPETITION AND DEPRESSION

Still, if a troupe had the ability, its members generally preferred to stay in London. It was more comfortable to remain in the same city from one day to the next; certainly the actors appreciated the stability of being at home with their families. It was also easier for a troupe to deal with familiar audiences and theaters rather than to enter a new town every few days, uncertain of whether they would be welcomed and where they might perform. And of course, London was the center of English society, politics, commerce, and culture. Both economically and artistically, it was the best place in the country for a group of actors.

Companies thus vied with each other to capture a share of the London playgoing market. Although a few well-known troupes, notably the King's Men, had a strong foothold in London, others came and went. Occasionally, a

ELIZABETHAN LONDON: A CENTER OF INFLUENCE

brand-new company would come into town, strike a deal with a theater owner, and put on shows good enough to lure audiences accustomed to watching other groups. Conversely, well-established theater companies sometimes grew old and stale, and Londoners tired of watching the same actors, plays, and special effects. Troupes faced with dwindling attendance were often forced to either disband or to go on tour until the time seemed ripe for a return. Many chose the latter.

The political and economic situation in London sometimes pushed companies to go on the road, too, even if they would have preferred to stay in town. Although London officials strongly disapproved of plays during Elizabethan times, they usually permitted the actors to perform without too much interference. At times, though, the government cracked down. In 1597, for example, the lord mayor of London complained that plays were "a special cause of corrupting youth,"[88] and promised to tear down all the theaters. In the end, the government did not carry out the mayor's threat, but several actors and theater owners were jailed; and before long, nearly all the London-based companies had ventured into the provinces.

Economic depression was another concern. The theater companies made their profits by attracting customers, and men and women who could not afford to pay did not come to the show. During prosperous times in London, the troupes made money, but when wages fell and prices rose, companies often left town. Although conditions were not necessarily better in the provinces, anything was worth a try when most Londoners were forced to spend what little money they had on food and shelter.

PLAGUE

But the biggest reason why London companies took to the road involved disease. Highly contagious and very deadly, epidemics of bubonic plague struck London several times during the Elizabethan era and immediately afterward. When plagues arose, officials usually closed the theaters. Part of the reason was medical: since plague was spread by close contact, it made sense to keep people away from places where they would be packed tightly together. But religious morality played a role, too. Puritan officials, in particular, routinely interpreted the outbreaks as a sign of God's anger, sparked by "the inordinate haunting of great multitudes of people . . . to plays, interludes, and shows."[89]

Whatever the reason for the closures, plagues darkened all London theaters until the epidemic had run its course. The worst of these outbreaks, from a theatrical standpoint, was probably the one that struck London in the fall of 1592. The spread of the disease canceled all performances until June 1594, except for a brief period in the winter of 1593. But shorter suspen-

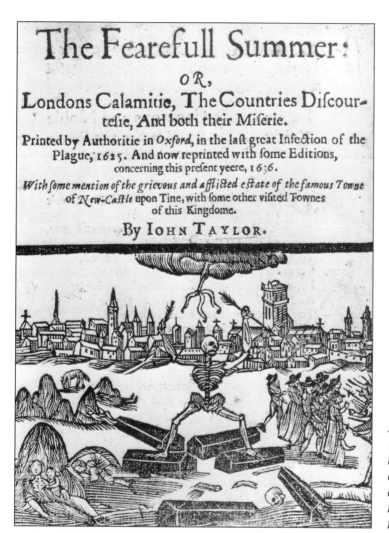

The Fearefull Summer:
OR,
Londons Calamitie, The Countries Difcour-
tefie, And both their Miferie.

Printed by Authoritie in *Oxford*, in the laft great Infection of the
Plague, 1625. And now reprinted with fome Editions,
concerning this prefent yeere, 1636.

*With fome mention of the grievous and afflicted eftate of the famous Towne
of New-Caftle upon Tine, with fome other vifited Townes
of this Kingdome.*

By IOHN TAYLOR.

A book published in 1636 describes the terrible plague that overtook London. One effect of the disease was to radically diminish theater attendance.

sions of productions were common as well. A 1604 license issued to Queen Anne's Men, for example, specified that they could only begin to perform "when the infection of the plague shall decrease to the number of thirty weekly within our city of London."[90] Thirty cases of plague a week was not a lot in a city the size of London, but it was enough to close down the theaters.

The best response the companies had to plague outbreaks was to travel. They hoped to continue to perform in areas of the country where the plague had not yet spread and thus stay in business. That was usually possible. Unlike the so-called Black Death of the fourteenth century, the plagues of Elizabethan times did not sweep across all of England. However, the strolling players sometimes ran afoul of suspicious local authorities during the plague years. In 1624, the city of Norwich forbade a group of actors from entering the community, fearing that the troupe might be carrying the virus.

Going on tour had another practical benefit for the players: It allowed them to escape contagion themselves. The best defense against the plague was to leave the site of greatest infection. Actors were no more immune to the plague than other Londoners, and most eagerly accepted the opportunity to escape. Unfortunately, they were unable to bring their families with them. Sometimes the consequences of that were disastrous. "Robert Brown's wife . . . and all her children and household [servants] be dead,"[91] reads a 1593 letter about the family of one actor who was on tour.

Still, there were good reasons to leave town when the plague struck. Even if an actor somehow avoided catching the disease, London was a dreadful place to be during an epidemic. "The loud groans of raving, sick men," wrote playwright Thomas Dekker in 1603, describing an outbreak, "the struggling pangs of souls departing . . . servants crying out for masters, wives for husbands, parents for children, children for their mothers."[92] It was better, Dekker concluded, to be as far out of town as possible.

TRAVEL

Travel was not easy during Elizabethan times, and it was even more difficult for the troupes that went on tour. English roads were unpaved and bumpy, a sea of mud in the springtime, dusty during dry summers, and frozen when the weather turned cold. Leading actors rode from one town to the next on horseback if they could afford it, but most of the company trudged along on foot.

Worse, the troupes also had to bring along a supply of costumes, set pieces, and other materials for their performances. These goods traveled in a small wagon, which was pulled along the rutted roads by animals, if the actors could afford it, and by the men themselves, if they could not. The players took great pains with these supplies, since they represented the company's major assets. Costumes, reported a player, were carefully "folded up with the thread, not against the thread."[93] Even so, the wear and tear on the materials was enormous.

The entourage spent their nights camped by the side of the road or at inns. The inns were of varying quality. Some were filthy and smelly. An Elizabethan who had stayed in many of these inns once published his suggestions for killing the fleas and other vermin that infested the rooms. "Fill a dish with goat's blood and set the same by the bed," he advised as one of his methods, "and all the fleas will come to it."[94] The traveling actors often found themselves in establishments where such instructions were useful.

At other inns, the proprietors were in league with the local highwaymen— thieves who traveled the roads in search of victims. These innkeepers secretly alerted the highwaymen to the arrival of guests who appeared worth robbing. Shakespeare included a similar scene in his play *Henry VI, Part 1*. It is possible that Shakespeare himself had been robbed through such a scheme; even if he had not been robbed, the odds are good that a crooked innkeeper had victimized at least one actor of Shakespeare's acquaintance in just this way.

But some inns, in comparison, were palatial. In the larger communities such as Gloucester and Bath, many inns were large and relatively sanitary. As one observer said, Elizabethan actors at these establishments were "sure to lie in clean sheets, wherein no man hath lodged since they came from the

A highwayman robs some hapless victims. Traveling actors were often accosted by such criminals.

laundress."[95] These comfortable accommodations tended to be used by the wealthiest London companies, rather than by the myriad of smaller troupes that crisscrossed England hoping to earn a little money each day.

LICENSES AND ROUTES

Before setting out to perform, touring companies needed to obtain a license to travel. Without official permission from a patron, usually a lord or member of the royal family, the troupe was subject to arrest and imprisonment. Getting a license does not seem to have been difficult for most reputable companies. A typical permit for the King's Men, signed by King James in 1603, allowed the group to perform in any "convenient places within . . . any other city [that is, besides London], university, town, or borough within our said realms and dominions."[96] Even though getting a license was a formality, it was still a requirement.

A handful of the touring companies set out on the road with a specific route in mind. Although no map or itinerary survives today, it is clear from several sources that the biggest London companies knew more or less where they were heading before they began. In 1593, for example, Edward Alleyn detailed his next few stops in a letter to his wife. "If you send any more letters," he instructed her, "send [them] to me by the carriers of Shrewsbury or to West Chester or to York to be kept

until my [troupe] shall come."[97] While Alleyn may not have known precise dates of arrival, he did know where his troupe was going.

Most traveling players, however, did not start off their journeys with a set itinerary. Instead, they went wherever they felt they could draw the biggest crowds—thereby mapping out routes that varied from day to day as well as from year to year. From long experience, the actors knew which communities were most receptive to strolling players. For example, the town of Bath in southern England was widely considered to be a good place to visit. The people were relatively well off, the government was sympathetic to actors, and audiences flocked to see the shows. In 1597, at least five major companies came through and presented a total of fifteen productions or more.

But the troupes did not meet with enthusiasm everywhere they went. Many towns were either too small or too poor to support a sufficient audience. Nor were all provincial governments as tolerant of players as was Bath's. In Marlborough, west of London, local law actually forbade plays from being performed. Technically, the players' travel licenses superseded these restrictions, especially if they were signed by a king or an important nobleman. But in practice, few players raised a fuss when they were denied permission to perform. It was easier to head down the

❧ EDWARD ALLEYN WRITES HOME ❧

While on tour with Lord Strange's Men in 1593, Edward Alleyn wrote several loving letters home to his wife, Joan, whom he affectionately nicknamed Mouse or occasionally Jug. This excerpt, quoted in English Professional Theatre, 1530–1660, *is typical in that it shows a keen interest in what was happening at home, and a strong desire on the part of Alleyn to keep in touch.*

Mouse, you send me no news of any things. You should send of your domestical matters, such things as happen at home, as how your distilled water proves [turns out], or this or that or any thing, what you will [want]. And Jug I pray you, let my orange tawny stockings of woolen be dyed a very good black against [before] I come home, to wear in the winter. You send me not word of my garden, but next time you will: but remember this in any case, that all that bed which was parsley, in the month of September you sow it with spinach, for then is the time. I would do it myself but we shall not come home till All Hallowtide. And so, sweet mouse, farewell, and brook our long journey with patience.

road in search of a more hospitable community.

Acting troupes did their best to avoid towns such as Marlborough, but doing so was hard. Economic and political situations could change dramatically from year to year. Prosperity, in particular, was often fleeting. People impoverished by a drought would not come to see a show, even though they had been eager customers the year before. Governments changed, too. One mayor might detest players, although his predecessor had welcomed them. There was often no way to tell for certain until a company actually arrived in the town.

The final consideration in choosing towns was the presence of other companies in the region. It was not profitable for a company to arrive in a community two or three days after a competitor. The prospective audience would be weary of plays and possibly out of money as well. On the other hand, it was good to be the first to play a certain town. But again, since communications were poor, it was difficult to know in advance whether a town was ripe for a performance.

PERMISSION

Troupes wishing to perform on the road had to begin by convincing the local authorities to give them permission. Their first stop, therefore, was always the same. "When players of interludes come to town," wrote a citizen of

Gloucester, "they first attend the Mayor to inform him what nobleman's servants they are and so to get license for their public playing."[98] During this interview, the actors did their best to portray themselves in a positive light, especially if they were a little-known troupe. Assurances that they were upright, respectable people often helped to win the companies the permission they sought.

However, the answer was not always what the troupes hoped to hear. As in Marlborough, many towns were deeply suspicious of actors. Puritanism was one main reason. In the provinces, religious sentiment against plays tended to be stronger than in the capital. Sometimes, too, the religious concerns merged into the practical. The presentation of a play encouraged local citizens to take time off from work and to spend their money. Some government officials disliked the idleness and the cost on moral grounds. Others worried that the plays would ultimately damage the community's prosperity.

Suspicion of the actors also caused authorities to turn away many troupes. Local officials often assumed the worst of the players. They were thieves, or only a little bit better; they did not obey standard ideas of morality; they were downright evil. One nervous official warned of "bad persons . . . wandering about the country."[99] In this view, the actors' presence would surely bring evil into the community, and they ought to be resisted at all costs.

In fact, there was a certain amount of truth in the charge. For many years, the provinces of England had dealt with strolling entertainers—among them dancers, puppeteers, and acrobats—whose shows were merely fronts for their real intention: creating trouble. Some swindled the population, others stole anything they could, and still others picked fights and drank to excess. A few of the players in the smallest traveling companies followed in this long tradition of criminal behavior and hooliganism. The bigger companies, of course, were much more professional. But the reputation earned by the few tainted all troupes equally.

And whether they intended it or not, the arrival of the players often created disturbances in town. In Ludlow, several drunken toughs broke into one performance and beat up the police officer on duty. A denial of a group's request to perform in Chester during 1615 mentioned "the many disorders which by reason of plays [create a] great disturbance [for] quiet and well-disposed people."[100] And in Southampton, a near riot after one production resulted in the destruction of most of the town hall's furniture. The Southampton incident was deemed so "hurtful, troublesome and inconvenient"[101] that town officials took no chances: Although the players were not directly at fault, acting troupes were banned from the town for several years.

Indeed, the possibility of violence so unnerved a number of communities that they actually offered the players money to go away. "Given to two companies of players which were not suffered [permitted] to play," reads an entry in a 1616 record book from Plymouth, "to rid them out of town[,] 30 shillings."[102] How common this practice was is unclear, but it happened on several occasions to virtually every important touring group. Less clear is whether the local officials gave the money out of compassion or out of fear; there is some evidence to support each possibility.

THE PERFORMANCE

If a troupe successfully made its case before the mayor, it was allowed to perform. Productions took place in a variety of buildings. Few towns had anything resembling the fine London theaters, but most had town halls, school buildings, or inns that could serve as acceptable substitutes. The troupes agreed

A traveling acting troupe comes to town. Actors were often regarded with suspicion by local authorities and, in fact, sometimes caused rowdy disturbances.

to stay for a certain number of days, sometimes only one but occasionally for as long as two weeks. Then they moved in with their costumes and set pieces and prepared for the show.

The first performance was always free of charge, and it was given specifically for the city officials and their guests. By tradition, the guests included many of the town's poor. "That [performance] is called the Mayor's play," wrote the man from Gloucester. "Everyone that will [wants to] comes in without money, the Mayor giving the players a reward he thinks fit to show respect unto them."[103] Hoping to impress the mayor, the players put all their energy into this performance. The better they did, the more generous the mayor would be.

Once the mayor's play was over, the players gave regular daily performances from their repertory. Sometimes the proceeds were divided evenly between the theater owners and the players themselves, just as in London. In other cases, the towns paid the troupes a flat fee for a certain number of performances. The financial risk was thus entirely on the side of the local governments. On the other hand, the fees the players received were relatively low. That was especially true if the troupes were unknown. Around 1600, for example, the town of Coventry paid small traveling companies about ten shillings per performance—but the much bet-

ter known Queen's Men received thirty shillings.

The citizens of most towns welcomed the traveling players. The shows provided them a break from their daily routines. The London companies, in particular, gave the people of the provinces a chance to see the best actors and the newest plays that the Elizabethan period had to offer. So great was the enthusiasm for traveling shows in one city that the local council had to replace the iron bar on a public building; it had been broken by "the press of people at the play."[104]

CUTTING CORNERS

However, it was rare for a provincial audience to see a play exactly as it would have been performed in London. Traveling was expensive, and companies that took to the road needed to keep costs down. One common method was to limit the number of plays they would perform. Instead of bringing along all the costumes and props they owned, the actors took along only those necessary to perform their most popular plays, or at least those they thought would be best received in the smaller cities and towns of England. Most troupes probably presented only four or five plays while on tour; however, one company, the Salisbury Court Players, took to the road in 1634 with fourteen plays.

Traveling actors perform in an inn yard. Performances outside London were far less elabo-rate than those staged in the city.

Moreover, companies performed with a much smaller cast than was typical for London. Every man who came along needed meals, sleeping accommodations, and a salary. Thus, troupes left many of their hired men in London. Failure to do so often resulted in financial disaster. "Our company is great [large]," complained one member of Strange's Men in 1591, "and thereby our charge intolerable, in traveling the country."[105] Apparently it did not occur to this troupe to cut expenses by leaving some of the men at home.

Others, however, did exactly that. When Lord Derby's Men took to the road in 1611, only fourteen men came along. Lady Elizabeth's Company, similarly, numbered sixteen when it toured the provinces a few years later. The reduction of men, of course, would have had a major impact on the quality of the productions. With fewer actors available, the troupes were obliged to

THE END OF PLAYS

Queen Elizabeth I was no Puritan, and neither were her successors, the kings James and Charles. But as time went on, the Puritan influence on English life and government grew. The impact on theatrical companies was great. In 1626, for example, during the second year of Charles's reign, a group of entrepreneurs tried to get a permit from government officials to build a theater. In large part because of Puritan disapproval, the petition was denied. Several years later, a number of Puritans banded together to try to get another theater shut down on the grounds that plays were immoral. Their attempt failed, but barely. The actors were increasingly aware of the threat created by growing Puritan influence.

But no one succeeded in actually closing down the theaters until 1642. That year, England plunged into a bloody civil war, sparked in part by Puritan distaste for Charles and his noble supporters. Afraid that large gatherings of people might prove troublesome, Parliament decided to ban theatrical performances temporarily. But as the war raged on, the revolutionaries slowly seized the upper hand. They used their authority to extend and strengthen the ban. A 1647 law forbade stage plays altogether, prescribing a whipping for any actor caught performing and a fine for anyone who watched. Two years later, Charles was beheaded, and the government, now ruled by a staunch Puritan named Oliver Cromwell, banned drama for good. Only in 1660, when the English rebelled against Cromwell and replaced him with Charles's son, did the theaters reopen.

Oliver Cromwell, a powerful ruler and strict Puritan, banned theater altogether in mid-seventeenth-century England.

rewrite or delete scenes altogether. The touring actors probably had to take on more parts than in London, too. Fewer actors also meant fewer hands to set up the stage, provide music, and deal with other technical issues of putting on the show.

But even with a smaller roster, traveling companies often had difficulty making ends meet. Proceeds were small and expenses high. Because so many towns barred their doors to the strolling players, there were too many troupes competing for relatively small audiences. Companies lowered their expectations and often their hired men's salaries as well: William Kendall's contract specified that he would receive "every week of his playing in London 10 shillings and in the country [only] 5." [106] But despite the cost cutting, most troupes did not make much money by touring.

And many went bankrupt. More than one company found itself broke and exhausted many miles from London. The Earl of Pembroke's Men, for example, set out on the road in 1593 but quickly ran out of money. "They are all at home and have been these five or six weeks," wrote Philip Henslowe, "for they cannot save their charges with travel, as I hear, and were fain [forced] to pawn their apparel." [107] With luck, the sharers of companies in this position would find a wealthy sponsor to redeem their sets and costumes. Otherwise, the troupe was effectively out of business.

PROS AND CONS

The inconvenience of traveling, coupled with the relatively low amount of money a touring troupe could earn, certainly created frustration for the strolling players. It could not have been easy to sleep in flea-infested inns, travel England during the November rains, and approach one town council after another with only modest hopes of a favorable answer. Nor was it easy for the actors to be apart from their loved ones. "And so, sweet mouse, farewell," wrote Edward Alleyn to his wife in one of the few surviving letters from a traveling player, "and brook [tolerate] our long journey with patience." [108]

Yet there were benefits in being on the road. In a time when few people traveled outside their own towns, the players had a rare opportunity to see their country. Touring also allowed the members of the troupe to get to know one another in a way that was impossible in London, where each man went to his own house after the day's work was done. "Since they liked and respected each other as human beings," writes Marchette Chute about Shakespeare and his fellow sharers, "they probably derived a good deal of enjoyment from traveling about the countryside [together]." [109]

And just as in London, the positive reactions of audiences no doubt made the hardships of the journey worthwhile. Unlike London audiences, the playgoers of rural and small-town England were not spoiled by regular attendance at the theater. As a result, the best provincial performances had a remarkably long-lasting effect on many members of the audience. As a small child in 1570, Robert Willis saw a traveling production of a play called *The Cradle of Security.* "The sight took such impression on me," he wrote seventy years later, "that when I came towards man's estate [death], it was as fresh in my memory, as if I had seen it newly acted."[110] To provide entertainment with lasting impact—whether in London or on tour—was the dream of every Elizabethan actor.

INTRODUCTION: "A KIND OF CONTRADICTION"

1. Quoted in G. Blakemore Evans, ed., *Elizabethan-Jacobean Drama.* New York: Meredith Press, 1988, p. 92.

CHAPTER 1: SHARERS AND APPRENTICES

2. Quoted in M.C. Bradbrook, *The Rise of the Common Player.* Cambridge, MA: Harvard University Press, 1962, p. 63.
3. Quoted in Neil Carson, *A Companion to Henslowe's Diary.* Cambridge: Cambridge University Press, 1988, p. 35.
4. Quoted in E.K. Chambers, *The Elizabethan Stage,* vol. 2. London: Oxford University Press, 1923, p. 115.
5. Quoted in Gerald Eades Bentley, *The Profession of Player in Shakespeare's Time.* Princeton, NJ: Princeton University Press, 1984, p. 49.
6. Quoted in Gerald Eades Bentley, *Shakespeare.* New Haven, CT: Yale University Press, 1961, p. 92.
7. Quoted in Marchette Chute, *Shakespeare of London.* New York: Dutton, 1949, p. 131.
8. Quoted in Chambers, *The Elizabethan Stage,* vol. 2, p. 297.
9. Quoted in Bradbrook, *The Rise of the Common Player,* p. 72.
10. Chute, *Shakespeare of London,* p. 246.
11. Bradbrook, *The Rise of the Common Player,* p. 162.
12. Quoted in Bentley, *Shakespeare,* p. 110.
13. Quoted in Bentley, *The Profession of Player in Shakespeare's Time,* p. 15.
14. Quoted in Carson, *A Companion to Henslowe's Diary,* p. 35.
15. Quoted in Bentley, *The Profession of Player in Shakespeare's Time,* p. 60.
16. Quoted in Chambers, *The Elizabethan Stage,* vol. 2, p. 329.
17. Quoted in Bradbrook, *The Rise of the Common Player,* p. 73.
18. Quoted in Chute, *Shakespeare of London,* p. 202.
19. Quoted in Chambers, *The Elizabethan Stage,* vol. 2, p. 305.
20. Chute, *Shakespeare of London,* p. 89.
21. Quoted in Bradbrook, *The Rise of the Common Player,* p. 73.
22. Quoted in Glynne Wickham, Herbert Berry, and William Ingram, eds., *English Professional Theatre, 1530–1660.* Cambridge: Cambridge University Press, 2000, p. 268.

23. Quoted in Bentley, *The Profession of Player in Shakespeare's Time,* p. 123.

24. Quoted in Bentley, *The Profession of Player in Shakespeare's Time,* p. 120.

25. Quoted in Chambers, *The Elizabethan Stage,* vol. 2, p. 44.

26. Quoted in Wickham, Berry, and Ingram, *English Professional Theatre, 1530–1660,* p. 264.

27. Quoted in Chute, *Shakespeare of London,* p. 127.

28. Quoted in Bentley, *The Profession of Player in Shakespeare's Time,* pp. 129–30.

29. Quoted in Bentley, *The Profession of Player in Shakespeare's Time,* p. 226.

CHAPTER 2: HIRED MEN

30. Quoted in Carson, *A Companion to Henslowe's Diary,* p. 38.

31. Quoted in Bentley, *The Profession of Player in Shakespeare's Time,* p. 111.

32. Quoted in Bradbrook, *The Rise of the Common Player,* p. 72.

33. Quoted in Bentley, *The Profession of Player in Shakespeare's Time,* p. 275.

34. William Shakespeare, *The Comedies of Shakespeare,* vol. 1. New York: Modern Library, n.d., p. 4.

35. Esther Cloudman Dunn, ed., *Eight Famous Elizabethan Plays.* New York: Modern Library, 1932, p. 436.

36. Chute, *Shakespeare of London,* p. 89.

37. Quoted in Bentley, *The Profession of Player in Shakespeare's Time,* p. 72.

38. Quoted in Chute, *Shakespeare of London,* p. 161.

39. Shakespeare, *The Comedies of Shakespeare,* p. 529.

40. Quoted in Bentley, *The Profession of Player in Shakespeare's Time,* p. 72.

41. Shakespeare, *The Comedies of Shakespeare,* p. 42.

42. Dunn, *Eight Famous Elizabethan Plays,* p. 143.

43. Quoted in Bentley, *The Profession of Player in Shakespeare's Time,* p. 89.

44. Quoted in Bentley, *The Profession of Player in Shakespeare's Time,* p. 93.

45. Quoted in Bentley, *The Profession of Player in Shakespeare's Time,* pp. 81–82.

46. Quoted in David Bradley, *From Text to Performance in the Elizabethan Theatre.* Cambridge: Cambridge University Press, 1992, p. 99.

47. Quoted in Bradley, *From Text to Performance in the Elizabethan Theatre,* p. 99.

CHAPTER 3: PREPARING A PRODUCTION

48. Carson, *A Companion to Henslowe's Diary,* p. 75.

49. Quoted in Chute, *Shakespeare of London,* p. 93.
50. Bradbrook, *The Rise of the Common Player,* p. 125.
51. Quoted in Glynne Wickham, *Early English Stages 1300 to 1660,* vol. 2. New York: Columbia University Press, 1963, p. 129.
52. Quoted in Chute, *Shakespeare of London,* p. 93.
53. Quoted in Wickham, *Early English Stages 1300 to 1660,* vol. 2, p. 128.
54. Quoted in Wickham, Berry, and Ingram, *English Professional Theatre, 1530–1660,* p. 129.
55. Quoted in Wickham, Berry, and Ingram, *English Professional Theatre, 1530–1660,* p. 102.
56. Quoted in Bentley, *The Profession of Player in Shakespeare's Time,* p. 84.
57. Quoted in Bradbrook, *The Rise of the Common Player,* p. 163.
58. Quoted in Chambers, *The Elizabethan Stage,* vol. 2, p. 297.
59. Chute, *Shakespeare of London,* p. 159.
60. Carson, *A Companion to Henslowe's Diary,* p. 74.
61. Shakespeare, *The Comedies of Shakespeare,* p. 494.
62. Quoted in Felix E. Schelling, *Elizabethan Drama 1558–1642,* vol. 1. 1908. Reprinted New York: Russell and Russell, 1959, p. 177.
63. Shakespeare, *The Comedies of Shakespeare,* p. 495.
64. Quoted in Bentley, *The Profession of Player in Shakespeare's Time,* p. 48.
65. Quoted in Chute, *Shakespeare of London,* p. 93.

CHAPTER 4: THE PERFORMANCE

66. Quoted in Bradbrook, *The Rise of the Common Player,* p. 111.
67. Dunn, *Eight Famous Elizabethan Plays,* p. 217.
68. Dunn, *Eight Famous Elizabethan Plays,* p. 216.
69. William Shakespeare, *Romeo and Juliet.* New York: Washington Square Press, 1992, p. 7.
70. Dunn, *Eight Famous Elizabethan Plays,* pp. 447, 489, 518.
71. Dunn, *Eight Famous Elizabethan Plays,* p. 581.
72. Dunn, *Eight Famous Elizabethan Plays,* p. 165.
73. Quoted in Wickham, *Early English Stages 1300 to 1660,* vol. 2, p. 310.
74. Dunn, *Eight Famous Elizabethan Plays,* p. 461.
75. Quoted in Schelling, *Elizabethan Drama 1558–1642,* p. 179.
76. Quoted in E.K. Chambers, *The Elizabethan Stage,* vol. 3. London: Oxford University Press, 1923, p. 77.
77. Ivor Brown, *Shakespeare in His Time.* Edinburgh: Thomas Nelson and Sons, 1960, p. 181.
78. William Shakespeare, *Macbeth.* New York: Bantam, 1980, p. 92.
79. Shakespeare, *Romeo and Juliet,* p. 247.
80. Shakespeare, *Macbeth,* p. 93.
81. Quoted in Chute, *Shakespeare of London,* p. 97.

82. Quoted in Evans, *Elizabethan-Jacobean Drama*, p. 82.
83. Quoted in Chute, *Shakespeare of London*, p. 42.
84. Bradbrook, *The Rise of the Common Player*, p. 99.
85. Quoted in Brown, *Shakespeare in His Time*, p. 137.
86. Quoted in Chute, *Shakespeare of London*, p. 70.

CHAPTER 5: ON TOUR

87. Quoted in Evans, *Elizabethan-Jacobean Drama*, p. 37.
88. Quoted in Chute, *Shakespeare of London*, p. 192.
89. Quoted in Wickham, *Early English Stages 1300 to 1660*, vol. 2, p. 82.
90. Quoted in Bentley, *The Profession of Player in Shakespeare's Time*, p. 182.
91. Quoted in Bentley, *The Profession of Player in Shakespeare's Time*, p. 202.
92. Quoted in Brown, *Shakespeare in His Time*, p. 80.
93. Quoted in Chute, *Shakespeare of London*, p. 193.
94. Quoted in Brown, *Shakespeare in His Time*, p. 90.
95. Quoted in Chute, *Shakespeare of London*, p. 195.
96. Quoted in Evans, *Elizabethan-Jacobean Drama*, p. 40.
97. Quoted in Bentley, *The Profession of Player in Shakespeare's Time*, p. 202.
98. Quoted in Evans, *Elizabethan-Jacobean Drama*, p. 41.
99. Quoted in Bradbrook, *The Rise of the Common Player*, p. 45.
100. Quoted in Bentley, *The Profession of Player in Shakespeare's Time*, p. 192.
101. Quoted in Bradbrook, *The Rise of the Common Player*, p. 115.
102. Quoted in Bentley, *The Profession of Player in Shakespeare's Time*, p. 190.
103. Quoted in Bentley, *The Profession of Player in Shakespeare's Time*, p. 195.
104. Quoted in Chute, *Shakespeare of London*, p. 22.
105. Quoted in Bradley, *From Text to Performance in the Elizabethan Theatre*, p. 70.
106. Quoted in Bentley, *The Profession of Player in Shakespeare's Time*, p. 184.
107. Quoted in Chambers, *The Elizabethan Stage*, vol. 2, p. 128.
108. Quoted in Wickham, Berry, and Ingram, *English Professional Theatre, 1530–1660*, p. 278.
109. Chute, *Shakespeare of London*, p. 194.
110. Quoted in Bradbrook, *The Rise of the Common Player*, p. 115.

FOR FURTHER READING

Anna Claybourne and Rebecca Treays, *The World of Shakespeare*. London: Usborne, 1996. Well illustrated and informative. Includes synopses and brief analyses of Shakespeare's plays, along with discussions of Elizabethan staging, acting styles, and dramatic history.

Horizon Magazine, *Shakespeare's England*. New York: American Heritage, 1964. Another well-illustrated introduction to Shakespeare and his time. Includes information on Shakespeare's troupes and the theatrical world in general.

Sue Lyon, ed., *Shakespeare's England*. New York: Marshall Cavendish, 1989. Picture book with detailed illustrations of England in the late sixteenth century. There is also information on the theater of the period.

Scholastic Inc., *The World of Theater*. New York: Scholastic, 1995. A short history of theater through the ages, including information on Shakespeare and the Elizabethans. Detailed lift-the-flap drawings, including a cutaway of The Globe, make this an especially appealing book.

Diane Yancey, *Life in the Elizabethan Theater*. San Diego: Lucent Books, 1997. A good introduction to the subject, including information on audiences, playwrights, and more. Sets theatrical information against a backdrop of the time and place.

Gerald Eades Bentley, *The Profession of Player in Shakespeare's Time*. Princeton, NJ: Princeton University Press, 1984. A readable and interesting account of actors and acting during the Elizabethan period. The book relies heavily on surviving documents of the time.

———, *Shakespeare*. New Haven, CT: Yale University Press, 1961. A biography of the great playwright. Includes information on theatrical conventions of the time and Shakespeare's role in Elizabethan drama.

M.C. Bradbrook, *The Rise of the Common Player*. Cambridge, MA: Harvard University Press, 1962. Traces the connections between actors and society during Elizabethan times, with particular emphasis on the changes in the way actors of the time were viewed.

David Bradley, *From Text to Performance in the Elizabethan Theatre*. Cambridge: Cambridge University Press, 1992. Focuses on how plays were prepared for the stage, with special emphasis on casting, plots, and the reconstruction of actors' movements on stage.

Ivor Brown, *Shakespeare in His Time*. Edinburgh: Thomas Nelson and Sons, 1960. As the title indicates, biographical information on Shakespeare placed in context. Includes useful information on theatrical conventions of the time.

Neil Carson, *A Companion to Henslowe's Diary*. Cambridge: Cambridge University Press, 1988. Philip Henslowe, a theatrical entrepreneur, kept records of his dealings with troupes and actors. This volume analyzes his records and draws conclusions from them about the theater of the time.

E.K. Chambers, *The Elizabethan Stage*. Vol. 2. London: Oxford University Press, 1923. Information about individual actors, sharers, and apprentices; attempts to trace the companies known to have performed during the Elizabethan era, with relatively little analysis. Can be difficult reading.

———, *The Elizabethan Stage*. Vol. 3. London: Oxford University Press, 1923. Focuses on theaters, staging, and playwrights. Also difficult reading.

Marchette Chute, *Shakespeare of London*. New York: Dutton, 1949. A readable if speculative biography of Shakespeare.

John Doran, *Their Majesties' Servants; or Annals of the English Stage*, vol. 1. Boston: Francis A. Niccolls, n.d. An overview of English theater from its origins to the early eighteenth century, with information on Elizabethan theater.

Esther Cloudman Dunn, ed., *Eight Famous Elizabethan Plays.* New York: Modern Library, 1932. Texts of several well-known plays, including John Webster's *The Duchess of Malfi* and Ben Jonson's *Volpone, or The Fox.* Includes a brief introduction.

G. Blakemore Evans, ed., *Elizabethan-Jacobean Drama.* New York: Meredith Press, 1988. Documents from the theatrical and wider world of the time. Includes commentary. Some of the records presented in the book are very interesting.

Felix E. Schelling, *Elizabethan Drama 1558–1642.* Vol. 1. 1908. Reprinted New York: Russell and Russell, 1959. Dated but nevertheless interesting look at Elizabethan plays, with a particular focus on the texts and the categories of dramatic presentation.

William Shakespeare, *The Comedies of Shakespeare.* Vol. 1. New York: Modern Library, n.d. Eight of Shakespeare's comedies in one book.

———, *Macbeth.* New York: Bantam, 1980. Well-glossed edition of one of Shakespeare's finest plays. Includes a brief introduction relating to the Elizabethan theater.

———, *Romeo and Juliet.* New York: Washington Square Press, 1992. The Folger Library edition of perhaps the best known of all Elizabethan plays. Thoroughly edited.

Glynne Wickham, *Early English Stages 1300 to 1660.* Vol. 2. New York: Columbia University Press, 1963. Focuses on the years 1576 to 1660. Especially useful for information on theaters, staging of plays, and issues of licensing and censorship. Can make for difficult reading.

Glynne Wickham, Herbert Berry, and William Ingram, eds., *English Professional Theatre, 1530–1660.* Cambridge: Cambridge University Press, 2000. Documents pertaining to the history of theater during Elizabeth's reign as well as immediately before and afterward.

Erik Wikland, *Elizabethan Players in Sweden 1591–92.* Trans. Patrick Hort. Stockholm: Almqvist & Wiksell, 1962. Scholarly study of traveling troupes in Scandinavia.

INDEX

PICTURE CREDITS

Stephen Currie has written more than forty books, including *Life in the Trenches* and *Life in a Wild West Show,* both for Lucent Books. A veteran of amateur theater, he has performed onstage in a number of community productions and done technical work for many more. He has also helped to direct several children's shows. He lives in New York State with his wife and children. His son Nick's knowledge of *Macbeth* and *A Midsummer Night's Dream* was especially helpful to him in writing this book.